"We're So Big and Powerful Nothing Bad Can Happen to Us"

"We're So Big and Powerful Nothing Bad Can Happen to Us"

"We're So Big and Powerful Nothing Bad Can Happen to Us"

An Investigation of America's Crisis Prone Corporations

by Ian I. Mitroff
and Thierry (Terry) C. Pauchant

A Birch Lane Press Book
Published by Carol Publishing Group

A Birch Lane Press Book
Published by Carol Publishing Group

Editorial offices
600 Madison Avenue
New York, NY 10022

Sales & Distribution Offices
120 Enterprise Avenue
Secaucus, NJ 07094

In Canada: Musson Book Company
A division of General Publishing Co. Limited
Don Mills, Ontario

Manufactured in the United States of America

10 9 8 7 6 5 4 3 2 1

Carol Publishing Group books are available at special discounts
for bulk purchases, for sales promotions, fund raising, or
educational purposes. Special editions can also be created to
specifications. For details contact: Special Sales Department,
Carol Publishing Group, 120 Enterprise Ave., Secaucus, NJ 07094

Library of Congress Cataloging-in-Publication Data

Mitroff, Ian I.
    We're so big and powerful nothing bad can happen to us / by Ian
I. Mitroff and Thierry Pauchant.
        p. cm.
    "A Birch Lane Press book."
    Includes index.
    ISBN 1-55972-051-4
    1. Crisis management. 2. Industry—Social aspects.   I. Pauchant,
Thierry. II. Title.
HD49.M57   1990
658.4—dc20   90-2378
                                                               CIP

To my wife, Bonnie, and my children, Jason and Kaara, who suffered through my long nights at the word processor,

and

To the memory of Frederick J. Hertz, friend and law partner, who proved to all who knew him that a handicap can be made irrelevant to a rewarding life and who taught me many things, not the least of which is to see the forest for the trees.

Contents

Excellence • The Fallacy of Limited Vulnerability • The Fallacy of Business as Usual • Crises Are Not Solely Negative in Their Impacts

The Invisibility of Technology • Technologies Do Not Come from God • The Technologies of Habit • Championing the Challenging of Basic Assumptions

PART III—SOCIETAL GAMES

. . . there is today a widespread feeling that our technology, our capacity to alter the earth and the relations thereon, is out-stripping our ethics, our ability to provide satisfactory answers to how that power ought to be exercised. And there is the further feeling that even when we know, or believe we know, what would be the right thing to do, our social institutions, the bureau-cratic machinery of courts and agencies, are incapable of bring-ing it about.

None of these feelings is new, of course. The gap between technology and morals is a theme that runs from Prometheus through Faustus, Frankenstein, and the low-budget sci-fi films in which our meddlings with nature inevitably linger to harass or destroy us . . . The gap between morality and law has been play-ing since Antigone.

But it would be ironic to dismiss these laments because they sound familiar (almost every epic in human history has voiced them). Rather, the laments sound familiar because they are among the central, continuing problems of civilization. And however unoriginal, it may be no idle conceit to suppose that today things *have* gotten worse [emphasis in original].

Christopher D. Stone,
Earth and Other Ethics,
Harper & Row,
New York, 1987, p. 17

America is powerful and original; America is violent and abominable. We should not seek to deny either of these aspects, nor reconcile them.

Jean Baudrillard, *America*,
translated by Chris Turner,
Verso, New York, 1989, p. 88

The only question in this journey is: How far can we go in the extermination of meaning, how far can we go in the non-referential desert form without cracking up and, of course, still keep alive the esoteric charm of disappearance?

Baudrillard,
op. cit. p. 10

This is the reason for this journey into hyper-reality, in search of instances where the American imagination demands the real thing and, to attain it, must fabricate the absolute fake; where the boundaries between game and illusion are blurred, the art museum is contaminated by the freak show, and falsehood is enjoyed in a situation of "fullness," of *horror vacui*.

Umberto Eco,
Travels in Hyper Reality,
Harcourt Brace Jovanovich,
New York, 1986, p. 8

Introduction

The present book is an examination of a wide array of phenomena that, on their surface at least, appear unrelated. On the one hand, it is about the forces responsible for the creation of mega-crises or threats to the environment as represented by Bhopal, Chernobyl, or the latest, Exxon Valdez. For another, it is about the need for substantial change at every level and aspect of society. For still another, it is about the intrusion of technology into our very modes of thinking in such a manner that our concepts of what is real have been altered drastically, perhaps irreversibly.

Most of all, the present book is an examination of the gap between (1) our ability to acknowledge *intellectually* that significant if not radical changes are required if we are to manage our environment, and (2) the incredible denial that exists on the *emotional* level of the need for substantial change. It is precisely this gap that makes change so difficult. It keeps us from seeing that the more that things appear to be different, the more that, under the surface, they are actually parts of the same general phenomenon. This is our key point. The general failure to see connections between seemingly disparate things is one of the biggest factors responsible for large-scale crises.

. . .

At the time of the writing of this book, Eastern bloc countries are engaged in actions that a few short years ago, not to say months, would have been utterly unthinkable. They are reexamining, and in many cases rejecting outright, the socialist foundations of their political and economic systems. For the first time, there is open talk of experimenting with Western-style political and economic systems. For these and other reasons, it is more imperative than ever that we in the West look seriously at some of the foundations and consequences of our own systems.

In the waning years of the 20th century, it is no exaggeration to say that we live in a Business and a Media dominated society. What this means to our lives, and those of our children's children, is the subject of this book.

The book is divided into three main parts. Part I discusses the powerful and often tragic effects that Western business organizations have on the individuals that work in them. Part II discusses the powerful and often tragic effects that business organizations have on the environment with such major disasters as Bhopal (Union Carbide) or Exxon Valdez. Finally, Part III discusses the powerful and tragic (though often invisible) effects of the media-made American culture, which both shapes and is shaped by American business and technology. One cannot fully comprehend the impacts of business and the media on our lives independently of an analysis of American culture, the broader "fish tank," so to speak, in which we all swim.

Human problems are basically the same whether we encounter them at the level of the individual, the organization, or society as a whole because the same basic mechanisms and processes operate. Another way to put it is to say that the "craziness" found at each level is essentially the same.

Since we focus a good deal on this disturbance as a fundamental part of the human condition, it is therefore all the more important to point out that craziness *per se* is not our basic concern, even though we examine it in depth. Our real concern is the need for substantial change at all levels of our society if we are to avoid future large-scale disasters. Change and crises are the principal themes of our book. We are concerned with disturbed behavior because it is one of the most powerful forces affecting our ability to change as well as to prevent major crises.

One of the best ways to observe how business and government organizations affect individuals and the environment is in terms of *Crisis Management*. Crisis Management is a relatively new field, and for that reason one that is still struggling to emerge. It endeavors to understand how and why large-scale *human-caused* crises occur, and what, if anything, can be done to prevent them. This new field is extremely important because for the first time in history, humankind has the potential to create crises which can rival natural disasters in their scope and magnitude.

Large-scale crises such as Bhopal, the tragic explosion of the Space Shuttle Challenger, and Exxon Valdez unleash, as well as trigger, the best and the worst impulses in individuals and organizations. In the course of the over 350 interviews that we and our associates[1] conducted with top-level senior executives charged with overseeing crisis management for their organizations, we have come to appreciate a vital point: *How senior business and government executives thought about, conceptualized intellectually, and even more significantly, reacted emotionally to the possibility of a major crisis occurring to them and their organizations revealed more about them than all the rational studies of management and organizations.* How people react to crises and/or extreme events, both real and imagined, provides one of the most powerful windows, if not *the most powerful window,* into the souls of people and their institutions. As a result of our hundreds of interviews, we have witnessed both the intense fears and powerful defenses unleashed in people and institutions by crises.

To the best of our knowledge, major crises do not primarily occur because of the rational and intellectual limitations of people and institutions, although to be sure these are important factors. Rather, they occur primarily because of emotional and ethical limitations. To put it differently, major crises occur because of what students and practitioners of management alike have termed "bounded rationality," i.e., people and institutions are limited in the amounts and the variety of information and alternatives they can consider and process. It is even more common that major crises occur because people and institutions are "bounded emotionally and ethically." They are limited in their ability to acknowledge situations fraught with extreme conflict, anxiety, and uncertainty.

In the course of our many interviews, we found virtually no cases of individuals who were unable to "think" about major crises because of cognitive impairment or intellectual limitations. Nearly all of our interviewees had heard about Bhopal or any one of countless other disasters. They and their organization's inability to consider seriously

---

1. These include: Dr. Christine Pearson, Associate Director of the USC Center for Crisis Management; Research Associates Judith Clair, Michael Finney, Sarah Kovoor, and Maria Nathan.

the all-too-real possibility of being "hit" by a similar disaster or crisis was due more to the fact that they could not emotionally handle the extreme anxieties and fears that even the thought of a crisis raised. In a real sense, *they were too preoccupied with their own internal, emotional struggles or crises to have any energy left over to face external crises.* Such behavior is entirely understandable once it is appreciated that the vast majority of them had never received any professional counseling, or the appropriate formal education, to face such challenges. As a result, they behaved like most people who are unprepared to handle extreme situations. They (and their institutions) denied the need to prepare for major crises. As we shall see, they were exceptionally clever and creative in the rationalizations they devised to avoid having to consider and prevent the possibility of a major crisis.

One of our other principal aims is to correct faulty notions regarding organizations. For instance, a common misperception is that organizations are not creative, that they stifle and block the creativity of their members. Like so many, this misperception is only partly true at best. We have found, to the contrary, that organizations are vastly creative. The real issue is where that creativity is focused. Almost by definition, in troubled or disturbed organizations, the creativity of their members is channeled into dangerous or unproductive activities. The point is that human creativity has to be exercised somewhere. If organizations are not able to channel their creativity into productive activities, then it will go into activities counter to the purposes of the organizations and society.

For purposes of clarity, ease, and directness of presentation, we have encapsulated these reactions into various "games" that individuals, institutions, and American society as a whole become trapped into playing. However, make no mistake about it, by using the device or metaphor of "games," we intend neither to demean nor to trivialize the phenomena which are our main concern. Indeed, the proliferation and seemingly limitless consumption of "pop" books about serious subjects is itself one of the many central "games" that our society plays in the attempt to flee from a too painful reality that more and more of us fail to acknowledge, let alone do something serious about. By labeling what we have observed as "games," our purpose is, first of all, to expose them as such, and second, to show how to break out of them. As we shall see, the best organizations will be our guide. Though few in number, they are nonetheless our only hope for the future. The best show us how to break out of "games" by not getting trapped into them in the first place. Yet, even this finding must be placed in its proper context.

As a result of our interviews and additional studies in the area of Crisis Management, it has become clear to us that the prevention of major crises requires much more than merely "fine-tuning" current business practices. Instead, a revolutionary change in current management thought and practice is required. The reason is that major crises neither are caused by nor are the result of a *few* "bad" corporations, or "faulty" management decisions or principles. Instead, *the basic conceptions and principles by which virtually all organizations operate are inherently flawed and outmoded.* The so-called "bad" corporations merely embody these outmoded conceptions to a greater degree and hence allow us to see them much more clearly. The problems we face are much more severe than they appear at first glance.

Because we are so critical of current management theory and practice, it should be strictly understood that we are not opposed to business per se. Our objective is one of improving the role of business in societies everywhere. Our overall thesis is that business has lost sight of its fundamental purpose. The fundamental purpose of business is to create substantive knowledge, to develop new products and services for the advancement of society as a whole. Thus, the creation of wealth is merely the means to these ends and never the end in itself. When businesses everywhere lose sight of the proper ends, they trigger industrial disasters and major crises, threaten the natural environment, and impoverish and alienate the people connected with them.

At the very time in our history when Eastern bloc countries are rejecting socialism, we cannot in good conscience recommend the wholesale adoption of Western-style forms of organization without noting their serious deficiencies and acting seriously to correct them. Capitalist-style organizations need not be perfect in order that they be both recommended and preferred. But surely, they cannot be adopted under the delusion that they are free from serious defects. Self-criticism has always been touted as one of the distinctive hallmarks of free societies everywhere. This fundamental feature is hollow indeed if we are not free to critique ourselves, especially when it is not only long overdue, but desperately needed.

Finally, this book is an exploration of the multitude of ways in which technology is altering the very nature of individual consciousness, large institutions, and even society itself. Many of the crises that we have seen in the last decade have something to do, either directly or indirectly, with the ubiquitous presence of technology in our lives.

In the end, the message is not that we should abandon all technology and thereby return to some "natural state" of existence. Rather, the message is that we need to change our ways of thinking about managing technology as fundamentally as technology is changing us. We need in other words to make the invisible visible and to see how many disparate and hidden factors affect our ability to manage our lives.

Part I

PEOPLE GAMES

Chapter 1

The Codependencies of Corporations

We have begun to recognize that many of the behaviors considered "normal" for individuals and organizations are actually a repertoire of behaviors of an active addict or nonrecovering codependent [e.g., alcoholic]. For example, the solutions [often recommended for American business to improve its competitiveness such as ruthlessness, rigidity, dishonesty] are exactly the ways that an active drunk would respond to crisis. In addition, many of the organizational processes deemed "acceptable" in companies are just more of the same addictive behavior masquerading as corporate structure and function.

Anne Wilson Schaef and Diane Fassel,
*The Addictive Organization: Why We Overwork,
Cover Up, Pick Up the Pieces, Please
the Boss, and Perpetuate Sick Organizations*,
Harper & Row, New York, 1988

. . . The great systems are headless, they have no protagonist and they do not live in individual egoism, either. Therefore they cannot be struck by killing the king; they are struck when they are made unstable through acts of harassment, exploiting their own logic: If there exists a completely automated factory, it will not be upset by the death of the owner but rather by erroneous bits of information inserted here and there, making work hard for the computers that run the place.

Umberto Eco,
Travels in Hyper Reality,
Harcourt Brace Jovanovich,
New York, 1986, p. 115

Over the past ten years, American culture and American institutions have been subjected to the most intense scrutiny and criticism in perhaps our entire history. Literally, a ton of books and articles have been written proclaiming that our business organizations and institutions are not only seriously outmoded, but basically have become dinosaurs. Where once our organizations and institutions were extremely well suited to a world in which we were kings, these very same organizations and institutions are now part of one of our biggest problems: our inability to change significantly enough to compete in the global economy. Particularly distressing is the fact that the research evidence upon which these charges are founded, while not perfect, indicates, nonetheless, a strong and persistent pattern.[1] In sum, the charges are that unless U.S. business "really gets with it," we are well on our way to becoming a *permanent* second-rate economic power.

Signs for this, both big and small, are all around us. Consider for instance the October 1989 San Francisco earthquake. It is projected that it will be the most costly disaster in American history. The billions it will take to rebuild the San Francisco Bay Area will be largely financed through the sale of U.S. Treasury notes to Japan. Increasingly, the Japanese not only buy our real estate, our banks, our entertainment and other industries, but they also finance the rebuilding of our destroyed and decaying infrastructure—much as we did for Japan at the end of World War II. The Japanese not only own what's on the surface of the U.S. but increasingly what's under it as well!

Most discouraging of all, instead of responding with an acute sense of national urgency, the latest studies and surveys continue to show that the majority of U.S. companies have responded with an attitude of "business as usual." Even worse, those companies which have adopted and incorporated the latest manufacturing technologies

---

1. See Ian I. Mitroff, *Business Not as Usual, Rethinking Our Individual, Corporate, and Industrial Strategies for Global Competition*, San Francisco: Jossey-Bass Publishers, 1988.

and, as a result, produced new products capable of competing in the global marketplace have, for the most part, operated them with "an outdated mindset." Thus, whatever benefits might have been realized by new manufacturing procedures and technologies have not only been neutralized but largely negated. It can even be argued that many U.S. firms are even worse off than before. They invested so much of their time, energy, and resources in an attempt to change, but having realized so little from it, their deepest hopes and even their fundamental will to change may have been seriously undermined.[2]

Consider another equally disturbing and related phenomenon, the significant increase in the number and impact of *human-made* disasters that now have the potential to affect the entire planet (e.g., Chernobyl) or large regions of the globe (e.g., Exxon Valdez). What's especially disturbing is not only the impact that such disasters have but that they seem well on the way to becoming a permanent feature of our newly created landscape. The potential for large-scale disasters seems literally to be built into the very fiber and fabric of modern civilization.[3]

At its very best, the potential for such disasters is a major but unintended characteristic of modern technologies. At the very worst, such disasters are totally different from those we have experienced in the past. Increasingly, they are caused by people, not by nature. A Hurricane Hugo and a San Francisco earthquake may be bad enough in themselves but at least they are acts of God. They are caused by forces over which we have little or no control. They can be neither totally predicted nor prevented.

The case with people-made disasters is entirely different. In principle, what is caused by people can be prevented by them. While they are not exactly equivalent, the knowledge to create new technologies capable of influencing the entire planet (e.g., nuclear power) contains within it the germ of knowledge necessary to prevent disasters that are caused by them.

With the preceding thoughts in mind, it is instructive to consider an event at which both authors were present. In mid-September 1989, we were fortunate to have attended a major conference on crisis man-

---

2. John A. Young, "Technology and Competitiveness: A Key to the Economic Future of the United States," *Science*, Vol. 241 (July 15, 1988, pp. 313-316); S. S. Cohen and J. Zysman, "Manufacturing Innovation in American Industrial Competitiveness," *Science*, Vol. 239, March 4, 1988, pp. 110-114.
3. See Charles Perrow, *Normal Accidents. Living With High-Risk Technologies.* New York: Basic Books, 1984.

agement in New York City. The opening session, which occupied the entire morning, featured three major speakers: the lieutenant governor of the state of Alaska, the president of Exxon Shipping, and the head of the Coast Guard responsible for the waters around Alaska. The entire session was devoted to a discussion of the Exxon Valdez oil disaster, the spilling of over ten million gallons of oil in the Bay of Valdez, Alaska. The purpose of the session, if not the entire conference, was to ascertain what lessons, if any, have been learned so that in the future such disasters could be avoided. Space does not permit us to recount the entire discussion. However, the entire session is not even worth repeating in its entirety.

It hardly comes as any great surprise to learn that both the lieutenant governor and the head of the Coast Guard were much more open than the representative from Exxon to admit errors on their part and the lessons to be learned. Even here there was not as much progress as one would desire. It should also come as no surprise to learn that the president of Exxon Shipping, William Stevens, was nowhere near as forthcoming, given the fact that he openly admitted that the case would be in litigation for years. The major division/operating company of Exxon of which Mr. Stevens was president was responsible not only for overseeing the tanker Exxon Valdez but for managing the cleanup as well. For this reason, it is also not surprising to hear how Mr. Stevens responded to the following question put to him by the first author at the end of the formal remarks by the three parties: "Given that it is very rarely the case—*virtually never*—that the end link in the chain, in this case Hazelwood, captain of the Exxon Valdez, is *solely* responsible for the cause of the major disaster, what then is Exxon doing to examine the part that was played in the disaster by its management structure and organizational culture? In other words, in virtually every case of a major disaster that we and others have examined, the entire management structure and culture of the company has played a major role. Can you respond to this?"

Mr. Stevens responded by denying that Exxon's management structure or culture was at fault. Instead, he contended it was purely a case of individual human operator error. If culture was involved at all, it was the culture of crews and ships at sea.

At the closing session of the conference, Stevens was explicitly called a "fool" by one of the members of the audience, who, significantly, was not an academic but rather a corporate executive. It should be noted that corporate executives made up approximately half of the attendees of the conference. He was called a "fool" because it was not Hazelwood but executive management who, some weeks before the disaster, made the critical decision not to reexamine its preparations for a major spill because the likelihood of one occurring was judged to be too small to warrant further precautions. Besides, didn't the fact that there had never before been a major spill justify lowering the probability of a future one? A perverse variation of Russian Roulette was in operation.

What really raised the hackles of "some" (not "all" by any means) members of the audience was the angry remark made earlier by Mr. Stevens himself: "What would you have had us [Exxon] do, protect every single inch of the coastline of Alaska? That's patently impossible!" The answer to this question is of course "No!" But the very question itself deliberately covers up and obscures an essential point: One may not be required to protect every inch of a fragile coastline, but one is obligated to protect the most vulnerable point (every day two million gallons of oil flowed into and out of the Port of Valdez), a site that Exxon had promised to protect as a condition for being granted the license to operate in the region. Exxon had promised that the necessary equipment would be there both to prevent a spill from occurring in the first place and to clean one up in case it did occur. No, Stevens was called a fool because Exxon knowingly reneged on its promise. It cut back on safety and maintenance when oil prices took a sharp downturn on world markets. Safety and maintenance operations were judged to be the most expendable part for cutting costs from the entire operation. (It is believed that similar such cuts in safety were responsible for contributing signficantly to, if not producing, the conditions that resulted in the deadly release of gas that caused thousands of deaths on Bhopal, India.) Not only was the proper equipment not there in the first place, but what equipment there was, was improperly maintained and hence was dysfunctional. The fact is, the technology it would take to contain a spill of that magnitude does not even exist. In addition, it took untold hours, growing to a day and a half, to even start responding to the spill; this lag was due, not to Captain Hazelwood on whom blame was placed, but to the poor communications structure within Exxon, not to mention the faulty lines of communication and authority that existed both between and within Exxon, the state of Alaska, and the Coast Guard. This buck passing is one of the most prominent characteristics of Exxon's culture. It is also one of the most salient features of those organizations that, as we shall see, are Crisis Prone: their fundamental inability to tell and to admit the truth to themselves, let alone the world.

Instead of allowing the truth to come out, they suppress it or obscure it, worsening their reputation. They persist in communicating the belief that it is *they* who have been wronged, thus contributing even further to the very thing they continue without much success to combat, their appearance of arrogance. Thus, in a recent interview in *Time*, Lawrence Rawl, Exxon's company chairman, responded as follows:

> I've been with Exxon for thirty-eight years, and the thing that has bothered me most is not the castigation, the difficulties or the long hours; it's been the embarrassment. I hate to be embarrassed, and I am. Our safety practices have been excellent, and we have drilled them and drilled them into our employees over the decades. There is a lot of pride inside Exxon all over the world, and that pride is being challenged. We'll win it back, but we're not going to do it by debating on TV with some guy who says, "You know, you killed a number of birds." And we say, "We're sorry, we're doing all we can." There were thirty million birds that went through the sound last summer, and only 30,000 carcasses have been recovered. Just look at how many ducks are killed in the Mississippi Delta in one hunting day in December! People have come up to me and said, "This is worse than Bhopal." I say, "Hell, Bhopal killed more than 3,000 people and injured 200,000 others!" Then they say, "Well, if you leave the people out, it was worse than Bhopal."[4]

Two articles in the *Wall Street Journal* and the *Los Angeles Times* support the contention that the management structure and culture of Exxon were partly to blame for the accident:

> Industry experts as well as many Exxon insiders believe the company has a belated case of "restructuring blues," including a workforce stretched too thin, shaken management confidence, and sinking morale. Four years ago, to prop up its profits in

4. Richard Behar, "Exxon Strikes Back," *Time*, March 26, 1990, p. 63.

stock in the face of collapsing oil prices, Exxon eliminated some operations, peeled away layers of management, and talked many people into leaving. Ultimately, worldwide employment was reduced 28 percent, to 104,000 people . . . The cutbacks seemed to work, earnings and the stock price began recovering. But that was before the past year's series of mishaps.

Today, "the system is overworked and undermanned," contends William Randol, a former Exxon employee who is now a Wall Street oil analyst. Some Exxon executives candidly agree that certain operations are at least 10 percent short on personnel. Says one executive: "we haven't learned how to play with the thinner bench." He asked not to be identified.

Exxon's top brass admit concern. "Not everything we did in '86 was perfect," says Lee Raymond, President. He says that recent events "raise a fundamental question about discipline within the organization."

Exxon has begun an internal inquiry into whether anything is systematically wrong in the way the huge corporation, with annual revenue of $96 billion, operates. "We don't believe there is, but we're acting like there may be. We have no conclusions yet," Mr. Raymond says.

Chairman Lawrence G. Rawl, sprawling across a chair in his Rockefeller Center office, is more openly frustrated. The problem with restructuring, he says, is the human factor. "Can people perform the job they're given? You can't just test a person like a computer chip."

"Prior to the restructuring you were thrilled if you worked for Exxon; you were on top of the world," says William Hall, a New Jersey employee. "Now," he feels, "you're just a social security number."[5]

The more things change at Exxon . . . the more they have stayed the same.

More ominously, Exxon continues to spill oil and suffer other accidents, more recently at facilities on a waterway between New York and New Jersey. It's not clear whether the acci-

---

5. Allanna Sullivan, "Stretched Thin: Exxon's Restructuring in the Past Is Blamed for Recent Accidents, Cost Cuts in '86 Helped Profit, But Did They Make Spills, Refinery Fire More Likely?, Human Factor Worries Rawl," *Wall Street Journal*, March 16, 1990, p. 1.

dents are unique to Exxon or are merely the result of bad luck and bad timing.[6]

An article in *Fortune* put the matter even more bluntly:

> Where Exxon looks chiefly vulnerable is in leadership. Rawl and his team appear to lack the ability to understand people and to inspire them. Management has repeatedly underestimated public reaction to the spills and contrives to talk as though the public has nothing at stake. Rawl says he didn't go to Alaska at once because the clean-up was in capable hands and he had "many other things to do." An interesting point here: The earnings of his U.S. operations were going down the drain in Prince William Sound, yet he didn't rush to the site.
>
> By going to Alaska and acquitting himself while in the spotlight, Rawl would have accomplished two purposes: He would have reassured the public that the people who run Exxon acknowledged their misdeed and would make amends. And he might have salvaged the pride that Exxon workers once had in their company. Says one manager: "Wherever I travel now, I feel like I have a target painted on my chest." Employees are confused, embarrassed, and betrayed. Says an executive working in New Jersey: "The company is in turmoil. It's hard to get decisions. Everyone is studying safety in addition to his normal responsibilities."[7]

The behavior of Stevens stands in marked contrast with that of others who, when faced with crises of a similar magnitude, acted very differently. For instance, consider John Phelan, head of the New York Stock Exchange, and the featured luncheon speaker following Stevens. Mr. Phelan spoke forthrightly about what it was like to be directly at the center of a major crisis: Phelan was president of the New York Stock Exchange at the time of the October 1987 crash. When the U.S. economy was *literally* on the brink of a total collapse (if U.S. bond markets had also collapsed simultaneously, then the pos-

---

6. Patrick Lee, "A Year Later, Exxon Is Still Reeling From Alaska Oil Spill," *Los Angeles Times,* Business section, March 23, 1990, p. D14.
7. Peter Nulty, "Exxon's Problem: Not What You Think, The Embattled Oil Giant Is in Good Enough Financial Shape That It Can Almost Shrug Off the Cost of the Alaska Clean-up. But Morale and Long Term Leadership Are Another Matter," *Fortune,* April 23, 1990, p. 204.

sibility was very real that the whole economy could have, too), it fell to Mr. Phelan to go on national TV and not only explain to the American people what had happened, but assuage their fears as well. No small task! Before he did so, Phelan asked his top advisors to tell him the very worst that could happen so that he could tell the American people the truth as best he or anyone else knew it at the time. Given the stakes involved, the fate of the whole U.S. economy, it is difficult to believe that the potential for lawsuits was not extremely high.

In another case, the management of Perrier also acted forthrightly during their recent crisis. Faced with virtually a total recall of their products worldwide, Perrier admitted not only that the dangerous chemical benzene got into their products through the misactions of an employee who failed to change a filter, but also that the crisis was due both to individual human operator error and a management structure that had failed to detect it. In reintroducing the product, Perrier admitted not only that the crisis was due to individual human operator error, but that in addition, the company was reexamining its management structure in order to prevent such future incidents. Thus, we cannot explain in every case why one particular individual or institution is forthcoming and others are not as due solely to legal considerations. Given the litigious society in which we live, we take it for granted that the potential for legal action is high in every near and actual crisis. No, something more than legal considerations alone must be operating. And indeed they are. The factors are: (1) individual moral leadership or character, and (2) corporate character, conscience, or culture. This difference makes all the difference in the world. It is the disparity between the Exxons and the Union Carbides on the one hand, and on the other, a Lee Iacocca who, when faced with Chrysler's tampering with odometers on supposedly new cars, said simply and directly: "It shouldn't have happened; it did happen; it won't happen again!" End of case!

These two phenomena—the need for organizations (1) to change, to restructure themselves fundamentally so that they can compete in the new global economy, and (2) to change fundamentally so that they can lessen the potential for large-scale human-caused crises—are intimately connected. Every major crisis demands that something fundamental be changed; at the very least a serious reexamination of the organization should take place. Every significant change, whether at the level of the individual, organization, or society, sets off a crisis.

No significant change is ever accompanied without upsetting the comfort of the status quo. It is for this very reason that things often have to get so bad, i.e., turn into a major crisis, that people as a whole can no longer deny it. As a general rule, humankind prefers living with the anxiety of a known evil than the anxiety of a promised, but unknown utopia.

Because or in spite of our fear of change, one must ask nonetheless, *"Why can't we change?"* If despite our resistence to it, change is still the most naturally occurring thing in the world, why then do we fight and resist it with so much of our energies? Do we resist change so much because fundamentally down deep we are all irreversibly stupid, incapable of seeing and acting what is so obviously in our best interest? However comforting such responses may be, they no longer suffice.

In rejecting the traditional responses to the questions as to why it's so hard for us to change, we are not ruling them out entirely. They are just part, at best, of the full answer. Individual stupidity does operate. This is certainly bad enough, but organizational and institutional stupidity are even worse. Is it individual stupidity which somehow gets magnified even more in the process of creating and maintaining big organizations and large institutions?

Given the institutionalized stupidity with which we are constantly surrounded, this explanation is very appealing. Institutions *are* dumb, indeed, so much so that it is easy to find countless examples. Consider merely one.

THE FOOTLOCKER EPISODE

An alert, enterprising TV reporter for the local Los Angeles CBS television affiliate, KCBS, filmed a huge trash bin located behind a Footlocker store. The pictures were damning, to say the least. In the bin were scores of seemingly new running shoes that had been severely slashed so that they could not be worn by transients, vandals, etc. If one had intentionally designed a scene to show a corporation in the worst possible light, one couldn't have done a better job.

The reporter asked the obvious question on everyone's mind: "With the plight of the homeless so great in our society, why hadn't the store or the company donated the shoes to charities specifically set up to aid the unclothed? What, if anything, would the store have lost by doing this?"

At first, the feeble excuse, which itself had to be dragged from the company, was that the shoes were old, abandoned models and thereby might not be safe for use. Thus, to lessen the possibility of legal liability, the company not only disposed of the shoes but had them deliberately slashed so that they could not be worn. Later, however, the company seemed to realize its error and said that in the future such shoes would be donated to a proper charity.

How does one make sense of something that on its surface is so senseless? Who gave the order, issued the policy directive, wrote the memo, made the telephone call, or undertook the action, perhaps on his or her own, to destroy shoes that could have given warmth, comfort, and even a small piece of dignity to another fellow human being?

In itself, the event was not big. It was not a major news story. No one was killed, raped, or shot as is daily the case in Los Angeles. And yet, it triggered whatever traces of moral outrage had not yet vanished in the overwhelming volume of TV banality. Perhaps because it was so small, so sandwiched in between the big and the banal that appear on TV in no coherent order, it seemed all the more significant. It raised all kinds of questions. "Would a truly compassionate and moral society, let alone a single company, have allowed such things to occur?" If a company can be said "to think," what was it thinking, or better yet, not thinking, in order for something so small and yet so poignant to occur? Was it just part of the bureaucratic numbness and dumbness that inhabit present-day corporate America? Would a moral company not have done such a thing in the first place? The answer to this question is perhaps patently obvious. But what are the answers to other questions such as: Would a moral company have made hay of its donation of the shoes to charity, or would it have instead donated them quietly without fanfare?

The eminent American philosopher John Dewey once remarked that all problems begin with a human "felt need," i.e., the intellectual recognition that something was wrong and thus in need of correction. While logically correct, the Footlocker episode teaches us that this is not how important moral and social problems begin. Scientific and technical problems may begin with an impersonal "felt need," but human and social problems begin with a much more intense feeling of "moral outrage."[8] Social problems begin with such expressions as

---

8. See C. West Churchman, *Thought and Wisdom*, Intersystems Publications, Seaside, CA, 1982.

"How could we (they) ever have been so stupid as to do such and such?"; "How dare they (we) have done such things (or not done them)?" For instance, how could Exxon have allowed a captain with a repeated record of drinking pilot a ship in one of the most fragile and beautiful regions of the planet? Or perhaps they begin with just a simple exclamation such as "Damn them!" However they begin, how does one properly get a society to acknowledge let alone treat its important social problems?

INTO THE SOUL OF INSTITUTIONS

Because stupidity is so convenient and appealing an explanation, and because to a certain extent it does explain a great deal of human behavior, it is all the more important to understand that institutional dumbness does not occur primarily because of individual stupidity. Paradoxically, institutional dumbness occurs precisely because individuals are rather intelligent, not stupid. It occurs because, though we may be somewhat smart, emotionally we are all rather undeveloped.

We do not make the above charges lightly. They are the result of the over 350 interviews that we and our colleagues[9] have conducted with top executives of both public and private organizations. In the course of our interviewing top executives who were charged with the responsibility of preventing or managing major crises for their organizations, we began to notice that our results yielded a much greater insight into the general, everyday functioning of all organizations. Our interviews, which were originally conducted for the purpose of shedding light on a very specific matter—how to prevent major people-induced crises—actually shed light on a much more universal phenomenon: the behavior of individuals, organizations, and society, in general. Our interviews yielded a valuable side benefit that in many ways was more important than the originally intended purpose.

In many ways, none of this is surprising since psychologists have long learned that how people and institutions respond to extreme events or situations reveals even more clearly how they respond to everyday "normal situations." As a result of our over 350 interviews, we have learned that if some individuals are especially prone to accidents and crises so that we label them "accident prone," then the same is true of organizations. Some organizations can be characterized as a

9. See the full list of the names in the introduction.

crisis of huge proportions waiting to happen. We call these organizations "Crisis Prone." Other organizations, while not totally immune, have at least done everything humanly possible to try to prevent major crises from occurring in the first place and to manage better those that still happen. We call these organizations "Crisis Prepared."

During our hundreds of interviews, we encountered a number of attitudes in Crisis-Prone organizations that can not be explained by limitations in the abilities of both individuals and organizations to reason cogently or to think rationally. They have to be explained instead by emotional limitations. For example, a director of security at a large food organization considered that the "worst crisis" for his customers would be for them not to find his company's products on grocery shelves. This particular executive could not imagine the possibility that his company's customers could be poisoned by one of his company's own products. For another, during a major breakdown in technology, the director of public relations of a large telecommunications outfit relied on TV news for learning how her company's customers were faring. She could not understand the need to speak directly with her customers in order to understand firsthand and in depth the problems *they* faced. For still another, the director of a large oil refinery considered the worst crisis that could happen to him was not meeting his quarterly "budget targets" because headquarters would thereby scrutinize him more closely. This executive could not imagine the possibility that a major chemical accident could severely harm both his plant's employees as well as the broader community.

For another example, consider the head of public relations of a major oil company (not Exxon) who could not understand the fuss raised by Exxon Valdez. Echoing the sentiments of Lawrence Rawl, this particular executive stated, "No one was killed as was the case in Bhopal, so what's the big deal?" He went on to add, "The recent oil spill off the shore of California resulted in Huntington Beach being even cleaner than it was before." Apparently, the "logical" conclusion to be drawn from such perverse reasoning is that we should therefore have even more spills in order to clean up even more beaches or to infuse even more money into the economy of Alaska—this was indeed the case as the result of Exxon Valdez.

In interview after interview, it became clear that the limitations in both the ability to imagine and to manage the "worst" was not caused solely by limitations in the thinking or the cognitive abilities of senior executives. There was ample evidence that they could think well enough when they wanted to. There was also ample evidence that all of them had been exposed in one way or another prior to the interviews to a number of industrial disasters such as Bhopal, Challenger, Chernobyl, Tylenol, Exxon Valdez, etc. Theoretically, all of them were *cognitively* aware of the very real and ever present disaster potential of companies very similar to that of their own. Nonetheless, in most cases, they were unable to consider the possibility of similar crises happening to their own companies. Or, they were unable to empathize with concerns other than their own narrow interest or that of their company.

These findings thus suggested another type of explanation for the inability of far too many managers and top executives to think about crises. It became clear that the managers and professionals in Crisis-Prone organizations attempted to protect both the sense of identity of their organization as well as their own individual sense of identity as professionals. To admit emotionally that their organizations could experience a major crisis meant admitting that their company was not all perfect, excellent, and further, that they were not "good professionals." Or even worse, that the profession to which they had committed their entire lives, such as finance, marketing, or engineering, could be responsible for the widespread injuries or deaths of countless people.

As we said earlier, when a disaster of the magnitude of an Exxon Valdez occurs, rarely, if ever, is it due solely to the actions of a single, isolated individual such as a Captain Hazelwood, as Exxon would like to have us believe. In virtually all cases, a major disaster is the result of deep defects in the structure and the culture of the entire organization. For this reason, focusing all the blame on a single individual does not "fix" the real problem.

We have taken special pains in this book to emphasize the "existential" or the human, emotional side of crises. In a very real sense, the existential aspect stresses that if a major crisis has strong financial impact on organizations and their surrounding environment, which they certainly do, then a major crisis also triggers deep anxieties related to self-esteem, self-worth, and even one's basic identity. This existential side of a major crisis unleashes very powerful feelings of anxiety which lead most managers and professionals to exhibit a variety of defensive behaviors: the blanket denial of the very potential for a crisis. Such defensive mechanisms can in turn lead to further crises, setting off the need for even more powerful defense mechanisms, causing even more crises, and so on ad infinitum. This circular phenomenon creates what we call an "existentially based vicious circle," with tragic effects on both organizations and on their environment.

Notice that the anxiety produced is not "rational" in the traditional sense of the term. After all, one is not required to be an expert on all subjects or to be in control in all situations. The argument of "bounded rationality" that is thus stressed in so many texts on management does not explain fully such short-term protective (but long-term destructive) behavior. If such feelings of anxiety are thus "nonrational" in one sense, they are nonetheless very real in another.

In one organization we studied in the telecommunications industry, the head of engineering declared that the engineers in his company felt that their entire lives had been "shattered" as the result of a major breakdown in telecommunications technology. The breakdown not only adversely affected the firm's ability to transmit both voice and telecommunications for its customers, it also severely disrupted the sense that the company's engineers were "good professionals who worked for a good engineering company." The breakdown in technology forced the engineers to question the validity of some of their most basic assumptions about the adequacy of the kind of education they received in the process of becoming an engineer. Even more deeply, the crisis triggered deep feelings of anxiety with regard to their personal sense of self-worth.

To some extent, all crises trigger an "existential" crisis similar to a personal "midlife crisis." Basic questions emerge such as "Who am I?"; "What am I doing and for what reason?"; "What is my fundamental purpose in life?"; "Am I wasting my life in this job?"; or, "Can I understand and control the world around me?"

In order to survive the questions triggered by a major crisis, individuals often resort to a number of defensive strategies. For instance, some individuals "explain" the crisis away, pointing to factors that made it "special" or "specific," and in that way do not challenge their overall perspective or assumptions. Some blame others. Still others feel an urge to "engage in quick actions," "make hard and fast decisions," therefore refraining from the need to reflect on the meaning of the crisis before acting too precipitously. Some develop chronic anxieties which paralyze their ability to act. And others exhibit boredom or seem to shut down completely. Very rarely do individuals and organizations alike deeply ponder the meaning of a crisis, taking it as a fundamental opportunity both to learn and to change significantly.

We cannot overemphasize enough that our inability to face such challenges is not due solely to the fact that we are limited in our abilities to think and to process information. Our limitations in our abilities to handle the severe emotions that are unleashed by a crisis originate from deep defects in the "feeling structures" of individuals and organizations alike. *The fact that we are all "bounded emotionally" means that somewhat paradoxically neither individuals nor organizations can sustain long enough the emotional pain that is required in order to learn and to change. To be able to change significantly, one has to develop the capacity to feel and to endure enough pain!*

The present book examines how *bounded emotionality* affects individuals, organizations, and even our whole society, and what, if anything, can be done to break out of this vicious trap so that we can prevent future large-scale crises from happening.

Chapter 2

The Hecate Factor: The Myths Behind the Games

The assembling of a *commodity self* [emphasis ours], this "dream of wholeness," implies a sense of partialness and fragmentation that resides just beneath the surface. The appeal of style in 20th century cultures cannot be separated from the conditions of the human subject it addresses. We cannot, in evaluating the patterns of individual style, disregard the fact that over the past century, an ongoing lament has been that of aloneness, isolation, invisibility, and insignificance; a desperate thirst for recognition, often expressed as a desire for fame. A great deal of modern literature speaks eloquently of a crisis of the spirit; a condition of anomie and diminished meaning. *Amid the democratic puffery of the modern age, the self grows dimmer* [emphasis ours]. Behind these feelings lies a constellation of objective circumstances, the social world we inhabit.

The repeated pledge of *progress* [emphasis in original] is greater freedom for the individual, yet actual choice over the conditions of existence, the domain of freedom has been—in many ways—reduced. Nowhere has this narrowing of freedom been greater than in the modern structures of work.

Stuart Ewen, *All Consuming Images, The Politics of Style in Contemporary Culture,* Basic Books, New York, 1988, p. 79.

From our research and interviews, we have observed that there are at least two kinds of Crisis-Prone organizations. One we call "destructive," the other "tragic." Destructive Crisis-Prone organizations believe that it is their fundamental right to exploit any and all resources, whether they be human, financial, or physical, without any limitations whatsoever. Such organizations do not admit any wrongdoing or the necessity for change whatsoever. If a major crisis occurs, they are much more likely to blame others than to search for defects within themselves. These organizations seem to lack a basic capability of empathizing with others. They exhibit scant concern for issues of human dignity or ethics. Typical examples include the Ford Motor Company under the leadership of Henry Ford I, ITT under the stewardship of Harold Geneen, the Johns-Manville Corporation during the asbestos crisis. While we primarily feel anger and even intense disgust toward such organizations, even here we cannot fail to recognize and to understand what it is in the human condition that causes them to behave as they do. Indeed, we argue that we must understand such organizations even if all that we can do is to protect ourselves from them. However, to be as clear as possible, we are not condoning their behavior in the slightest. To understand evil is not equivalent to condoning it. Rather, if one would prevent evil, it is necessary to have some understanding of both its origin and its workings. The trick of course is to achieve this understanding without being contaminated by evil. Time and time again it has been shown that one cannot make repeated contact with evil without being infected by it.

With regard to tragic organizations, it is much easier to evince a feeling of empathetic understanding. To typify such organizations, suffice it to say that while they understand much of the necessity for change, they do not possess all of the structural, cognitive, and/or emotional resources needed for change to take place. In the following chapters, we will emphasize how such organizations are literally "trapped" or "stuck in their stuckness" due to their own structural and bureaucratic rigidity, resulting in the tremendous feelings of boredom and anxiety that their managers and professionals experience. Such firms typically cannot escape the necessity of "holding on to" the status quo. *They are incapable of managing organizational, industrial, and/or environmental change, let alone major crises, because they are overly absorbed in attempting to manage the personal and existential crises—boredom, depression, hate, anger, rage, drug abuse, suicide, etc.—of their own members.* It may be even truer to say that such firms are engaged in placing the major part of their energies in avoiding working on their own existential crises.

Traditional economic theory is not of much help in understanding large-scale crises or why humans do not change. The actions as well as the inactions of organizations cannot be explained by purely "rational" theories of human behavior alone. *If* organizations were rationally pursuing their self-interest over the "long run," *then* crisis management would already have been implemented if only for reasons of sheer survival. Something else must therefore be operating to prevent organizations from doing what is patently (i.e., rationally) in their best interest. The intellectual limitations of humans are thus only a part of the problem, at best. Deeper reasons are to be found elsewhere, in what we have called the emotional and existential domains of human behavior.

THE HECATE FACTOR

The myth of Hecate, the Greek Goddess of night, ghosts, and magic, gives us a powerful way of understanding those human forces which cause us to deny what is in our best interest. Through her general goodwill and power, Hecate once granted human beings material prosperity, provided eloquence in political assemblies, or assured prosperity in commercial activities. Gradually, however, Hecate presided over sorcerers and witches, thus using magic to will the general downfall of the human race and of all living things. From these great powers and purposes, Hecate has given us the term *"hecatomb"*: the large-scale massacre and destruction of humans and animals alike.

We have learned, particularly in this century, that the gods and goddesses of ancient times emanate from the deep recesses of our very own minds.[1] The gods are our very own, albeit unconscious, creations. They represent the attempts of humans to give explanations of the world around them in terms that are psychologically satisfying. Long before science existed, humans concocted stories based partly on their dreams and experiences to render the world intelligent in terms that people could grasp. An examination of Hecate is particularly relevant for a study of major crises since it sheds valuable light on how humans deal with crises from a psychological standpoint.

---

1. For instance, see Joseph Campbell, *The Hero With a Thousand Faces.* Bollingen Series 15, Princeton, NJ: Princeton University Press, 1949; see also Carl G. Jung, *The Structure and Dynamics of the Psyche,* translated by R. F. C. Hull. New York: Pantheon, 1960.

It is not coincidental at all that Shakespeare, in one of his darkest works, perhaps his best-known tragic and poetic drama, chose Hecate as the evil force that inspired Macbeth. Shakespeare provides us with perhaps the greatest crisis management lesson of all in brilliantly invoking Hecate in Macbeth's criminal deeds toward his kingdom, which eventually triggers his own death. Macbeth should be required reading for all MBA students. Instead, the current blame for crises, as treated in business schools, is placed simplistically on such factors as the unlimited desire for wealth, power, ambition, immoral and unethical behavior, or human error. While these factors certainly operate, Shakespeare's description of Macbeth's soul is more complicated and more fully describes the complexity of human behavior in relation to crises. While it is beyond our purpose here to discuss the play in depth, three aspects of Macbeth's character are especially pertinent. These three support our contention that in analyzing why both organizations and individuals get into crises, one needs to examine the "tragic" as well as the "destructive" aspects of the human condition.

To begin with, Macbeth was not driven by ambition alone. While in the beginning Macbeth murders the king for motives that are due to ambition, he nonetheless regrets deeply his act and is tormented by feelings of remorse, guilt, and even deep considerations of ethics. His regret, his disgust with himself, and his sorrow are so great and painful that it seems in the middle of the play that the attempts of the witches to cause his eventual downfall are bound to fail. Precisely at this moment Shakespeare introduces Hecate. Reprimanding the witches for not having consulted her before acting, Hecate modifies their strategies. Macbeth, she stresses, will not fall by ambition alone. She argues that Macbeth needs to feel an overpowering sense of security: "You all know, security is mortals' chiefest enemy" (*Macbeth*, 3:5). Notice that Hecate does not assure Macbeth of victory, glory, or success. She makes him believe that his personal safety, physical as well as psychological, will not be endangered whether he does good or evil, or whatever else is happening in the land.

Hecate neither gives Macbeth supernatural powers nor does she take away his free will. Throughout the entire play Macbeth struggles mightily with his own personal tragedy. He remains nonetheless essentially human as he witnesses the slow diminution of his being. Hecate does not dictate his fate. Macbeth is still able to steer his own destiny if he so wishes.

Through Shakespeare's genius, as spectators we can only empathize with Macbeth's tragic condition although we know he is both a murderer of wives and of children. While we condemn his crimes, we also recognize through him the fragility and the tragic nature of what it is to be human.

Macbeth is literally one of the clearest expressions of the differences between the "self-destructive" and the "tragic" individual organization. While destructive individuals believe in their grandiose dreams and ambition, and in their "supernatural" powers, tragic individuals are more likely to recognize their own fragility and limitations. Tragic people feel trapped, so much so that they despair of ever finding a way out of their difficulties. Destructive individuals also sense their loss of free will, but they consciously believe that they act by and for themselves. They are literally "driven" by their grandiose dreams. Further, destructive individuals have lost the capacity for self-reflection and the ability to empathize. In this way, almost like a psychopath, they do not experience feelings of guilt, remorse, or compassion. In contrast, tragic characters such as Macbeth, while committing crimes, remain aware of what they are doing. They both realize the possibility of steering their destiny as well as their basic incapacity to do so.

As an inevitable consequence, they become deeply alienated from themselves. They feel a profound sense of personal disgust and disrespect toward themselves, thereby losing in the process a basic interest in and a zest for life. Apathy and even indifference toward the absurdity of their own condition and of their entire life develops. They are neither "good" nor "bad." They lack the character and the emotional strength that would allow them to break out of the vicious circle of their own self-destructive behavior. Their main motivation is not merely to "win," as it is in the case of destructive individuals, but rather only to survive physically. Most of all, they seek an inner protection for their personal sense of existence and aliveness even though they realize that their existence is absurd and that their behavior will, ultimately, lead both to their own personal destruction as well as that of their community.

Hecate's work is indeed terrifying. The only hope she offers is the hope of eternal, everlasting misery.

MODERN UNDERSTANDING

While the Greeks, some 2,000 years ago, and Shakespeare, more than 400 years ago, provided astonishing insights with regard to human motivation, modern psychology provides us with additional evidence and insights.[2] This is not the place to give an exhaustive account of depth and existential psychology. However, in order to better understand the underpinnings of the various rationalizations and mechanisms of denial that we have observed in both individuals and organizations, we need to discuss some of the more important findings. In this regard, we are disturbed deeply by the fact that to an overwhelming extent these findings are not currently taught in business or engineering schools around the nation. Presently, most MBAs receive only a traditional grounding in what is called "organizational behavior," where the teaching of human motivation rarely involves more than a half dozen simplistic and trivial models of human behavior, complete with scores of boxes and arrows. All these models are so abstract and intellectual in nature that they are removed from the vast majority of human experience. For engineers, the situation is even worse; they don't even get these models in school.

Modern psychology indicates very clearly that the symptoms from which Macbeth suffered—alienation, loneliness, lack of interest in and no zest for life—all associated with his criminal deeds, are no longer the "privilege" of nobility. Quite literally, the "sickness of kings and princes" has been democratized. They are now experienced by millions of Americans, young and old, rich and poor, workers as well as top executives. Scientifically, such symptoms are referred to as "character defects." They are experienced as "a vague sense of not being real," "a feeling and sense of inner emptiness," "a lack of purpose and direction," "a sense of falling apart," "a lack of zest or joy for life," "feelings of fragmentation, of falling apart," "the experience of endless futility and boredom," "the sense of separation from society as

2. Carl R. Rogers, *A Way of Being*. Boston, MA: Houghton Mifflin Company, 1980; Karen Horney, *New Ways in Psychoanalysis*. New York: Norton, 1939; Heinz Kohut, *How Does Analysis Cure?* A. Goldberg (Ed.), Chicago, IL: University of Chicago Press, 1984; *The Analysis of the Self: A Systematic Approach to Psychoanalytic Treatment of Narcissistic Disorders*. New York: Inter University Press, 1977; *The Restoration of The Self*. New York: International University Press, 1977; *The Search For The Self: Selected Writings of Heinz Kohut*. P. H. Ornstein (Ed.), Volume 1. New York: Inter University Press, 1978. G. E. Atwood and R.D. Stolorow, *Structures of Subjectivity, Exploration in Psychoanalytic Phenomenology*. Hillsdale, NJ: The Analytic Press, 1984.

well as one's community," "a sense of alienation from one's life and work," "a lack of focus," or "a sense of fear and anxiety about one's future." Such symptoms are so much a part of modern society and are so close to the inner, intimate, and secret experiences of so many of us that, paradoxically enough, we can understand, to a certain degree, why most MBAs are currently not exposed to the literature which describes them. *The very experiences are often too painful to be acknowledged, let alone discussed.* Further, the teaching of abstract conceptual models that are far removed from direct human experience results in the denial of painful experiences by students and professors alike.

Technically, defects of character are referred to as "disorders of the self," or "narcissistic disorders." The term "narcissism" is not used here in its usual connotation. The term has a powerful negative association with "egotism" and self-centeredness. An important offshoot of traditional psychoanalysis has come into use arguing that there is a positive side to narcissism that is a state of "positive self-regard."[3] In this schema, narcissism permits individuals to experience feelings of inner strength, a personal sense of harmony and unity, and purpose, as well as the capacity to face the challenge of crises. Similarly, even the negative aspects are often misinterpreted! The traditional view associated with excessive self-love or overindulgence is contradicted by current findings. *Narcissists do not in fact love themselves enough!* In the depths of their psyche, those labeled in society as "narcissistic" are often people who are alienated and fragmented who have developed patterns of behavior that are dramatic, authoritarian, self-centered, and grandiose in an attempt to cover up inner defects, such as a profound sense of emptiness, for example.

One of the most important findings in modern psychology is that Westerners try at all costs to preserve their fundamental sense of "*self.*"[4] This is exactly what Hecate provided to Macbeth, a sense of inner security and safety, the confidence that his "personal sense of being" would be undamaged no matter what he did or whatever occurred in the world around him. The contemporary view of human behavior stresses that people resist with all their might anything that damages their secure sense of self and worth. Serious threats to the self are experienced as a feeling of disintegration. A void. Nonexist-

---

3. Kohut, *ibid.*
4. *Ibid.*

ence. Instability. Inner emptiness and lack of control, and power, i.e., the belief that one's "sense of oneness with the world" is shattered into a thousand pieces. Note that modern models no longer use dry and abstract language like "ego," "superego," "id," "drive" or "instinct." It is impossible to get in touch with that "id." The concept is far too abstract and removed from direct human experience. Yet, one can comprehend "feelings of fragmentation"—a sense of "not being all there."

The differences between a *healthy* experience of oneself and a *fragmented* experience are easily recognized. Some days we feel fine, energetic, and optimistic about life. It appears that nothing in the day can disturb our mood. We work fast and effectively. We believe in our basic capabilities and our sense of judgment. Our relationships with others are relaxed and fun. We forgive the shortcomings of others and ourselves. In short, we feel "put together," as "whole," as "one." Other days, however, are far less pleasant. These are the days where we spend half an hour dressing and undressing in front of the mirror because we feel that nothing "fits," arriving late at the office. We feel too fat or skinny, not tall enough, or much too tall. We don't like the shape of our nose. We find that it is difficult to concentrate on anything during the day. We lack focus. Our movements are awkward. We break things, we drop food on our clothes, we forget important events and make dumb mistakes. Often during such days we also suffer from aches and pains in our back, our necks, shoulders, legs, etc. Also, we have a low opinion of ourselves and of the world. People annoy us. We're short-tempered or timid. We find their personal views and concerns both ridiculous and ludicrous, or we envy them: the way *they* look, the way *they* talk, the way *they* behave. The future looks bleak and our jobs are boring. We are not just depressed. We not only feel fragmented, we literally are.

Writers in psychology and philosophy conceptualize so much in their writing, using difficult terms and concepts, that we cannot relate personally to what they are saying. As we shall see in the succeeding chapters, when we discuss the various games that individuals, organizations, and even our whole society play, we will see that they exist for the purpose of escaping the terrifying experience of "*death*." However, even here by use of the term "death" we do not mean it at the merely abstract or theoretical level. For most of us, "death" seems far removed from our day-to-day experiences, with perhaps the exception of people suffering from a grave illness, injury from a serious accident or the loss of someone close to us. When we refer to the experience of "death," we are not only referring to the actual time when we all die physically. We are referring much more to the *day-to-day experiences of fragmentation.* In this special sense, *death is more psychological than physical. Death here is experienced as a felt diminution, a disruption, a shattering, a fragmentation of our innate sense of experience, i.e., our basic sense of self.* The description above can apply to even relatively mild experiences. However, traumatic experiences such as a major crisis, or even the thought of its possibility, can awaken the strong, overwhelming, terrifying feelings of "death" that both destructive as well as tragic individuals and organizations all share in common. In such cases, the feelings of death will be so powerful that both individuals and organizations will attempt to preserve their basic sense of self in any way possible, including the use of rationalization and denial.

It would be a very grave mistake indeed to believe that such feelings are released only through tragedies of the magnitude of a Bhopal or Challenger. Through our research, we have uncovered identical patterns of denial and rationalization in crises that were much less visible or impactful. For example, during our interviews with executives, managers, and professionals that were affected by the 1988 Hinsdale telecommunication crisis in Chicago (a large fire disrupted a major telecommunications switching center that virtually shut down telephone activity throughout the Chicago area), we found evidence of similar existential traumas and, to a far less extent, the use of defensive mechanisms. For example, engineers who were involved in the disaster described later that their lives were "shattered" or stated that "it was like our whole life process collapsed." Managers who were affected by the crisis also expressed feelings of anger and isolation, or a sense of powerlessness and death. For example: "Hinsdale killed us; we felt we were caught with our pants down"; "We felt cut off from the world"; "It was almost a submarine mentality; I felt so isolated"; "Hinsdale was our umbilical cord to the world; afterwards it was a lot like a morgue." Similarly, the defense mechanisms that developed after this disaster were similar to those that were found after the Challenger accident. Some coped by "projecting" the entire fault or cause of the crisis onto the operating telephone company (Illinois Bell) or onto top management. They also included "disavowal" (i.e., downplaying the seriousness) of the economic importance of the crisis, which was later evaluated at some $300 million, and the downplaying of its sociological and psychological impacts. One executive stated that for her the telecommunication crisis was like "coming back to small-town America," before the telephone was invented. We also uncovered the use of other mechanisms such as "intellectualization." For example, some argued that similar crises could not happen in other locations, though the same kind of telecommunication switching centers exist throughout the entire nation.

We understand well the necessity for the use of such mechanisms. To give an idea of their tremendous strength, one has only to look at one of the most terrifying situations in all of human history: the Nazi extermination camps. Bruno Bettelheim, the noted psychologist and himself a prisoner in one of the camps, has written that under such horrifying conditions, people use a number of tremendously powerful defenses in an attempt to ward off their "psychological sense of death."[5] Bettelheim noted that some prisoners did not even dream of the awful events of death and mutilation that they had either viewed or experienced personally. Rather, they remembered and dreamt only about much more benign events, such as a guard pulling them by the shoulder. Or they dreamt of pleasant experiences that had occurred before they were in the camps. Others even denied altogether that the whole situation was real or was even occurring.

Such prisoners asserted quite seriously that the activities in the camp were in fact "staged" as part of a theatrical event. Still others developed a feeling of utter indifference to what was taking place around them or what was happening to them. In this way, they literally became zombies, that is to say, totally inured to whether they lived or died. This was the only way they could cope. The feelings of ultimate apathy that some developed in such situations are completely akin to the complete lack of feeling expressed by Macbeth when he learned that his wife had committed suicide.

It is also a grave mistake as well to believe that such people are "crazy." In fact, quite the reverse is true. Such people are in fact extremely creative in their development and use of techniques in order to preserve their sanity.

It hardly needs to be stressed that serious fundamental differences

5. Bruno Bettelheim, "Individual and Mass Behavior in Extreme Situations," *Journal of Abnormal and Social Psychology,* Volume 38, 1943, pp. 417-52.

exist between prisoners in death camps and managers in organizations, although one sometimes wonders. First, the death camps were designed specifically for the primary purpose of exterminating human beings. To be in one of the camps was tantamount to a death sentence.

Second, the prisoners in the camps were mainly (although not always) responsible only for their own lives. The case with managers in large-scale organizations is very different. They are responsible for the safety of thousands of fellow human beings as well as the environment at large. This is to say that if managers try to psychologically escape the reality of crises for personal reasons, they greatly endanger the lives of countless others.

CONCLUDING REMARKS

This chapter in particular provides us with the necessary background concepts to understand the various games that individuals, organizations, and American society as a whole engage in for the primary purposes of either not changing or not acknowledging crises. In effect, the games we describe in the following chapters exist for the fundamental purpose of protecting the fragile sense of self of individuals, organizations, and American society, and ultimately for justifying the status quo. Lest we be accused of overexaggerating, the best available evidence indicates that *at best* only 5–15 percent of all organizations even begin to approach what we call a Crisis-Prepared organization. The remaining 85–95 percent possess significant characteristics of those organizations we characterize as Crisis Prone.

As we shall see, all individuals to a certain extent engage in the various games we describe. Thus, a Crisis-Prepared organization that is more responsive to change is not one that is entirely free from all stress and anxiety. No single individual or organization has a completely healthy, developed sense of self. The complete willingness to change cannot be the criterion by which we judge people or institutions. Rather, the criterion is the ability to acknowledge their defects and to work on them. Healthy individuals, organizations, and even societies engage in the various games we describe in the following chapters but to a far lesser extent. More significantly still, healthy individuals, organizations, and societies do not merely play *unhealthy* games to a far lesser degree. They engage in totally different kinds of behaviors. These behaviors, if they could be called games, represent, as we shall see, a completely different set of "healthy games."

Chapter 3

The Games That Crisis-Prone Corporations Play

Let us consider this waiter in the cafe. His movement is quick and forward, a little too precise, a little too rapid. He comes towards the patrons with a step a little too quick. He bends forward a little too eagerly; his voice, his eyes express an interest a little too solicitous for the order of a customer . . . all his behavior seems to us a game. He applics himself to chaining his movements as if they were mechanisms, the one regulating the other . . . he is playing, he is amusing himself. But what is he playing? He is playing at being a waiter in a cafe . . . the waiter in the cafe plays with his condition in order to realize it. This obligation is not different from that which is imposed on all tradesmen. Their condition is wholly of ceremony . . . there is the dance of the grocer, of the tailor, of the auctioneer, by which they endeavor to persuade their clientele that they are nothing but a grocer, an auctioneer, a tailor.

J.P. Sartre,
Existential Psychoanalysis,
Chicago: Regnery, 1962

As we write, significant changes that would have been virtually unthinkable a short time ago are taking place in Eastern bloc socialist countries. Many are advocating abandonment of socialist governments and their associated economies in exchange for Western-style democracies and open, free market economies. For these reasons alone, it is imperative that we examine some of the weak spots of capitalism that can no longer be ignored so that countries everywhere can fashion the type of economies and organizations that will suit them even better.

Over the years, capitalist societies and organizations have been accused, often with much justification, of promoting a multitude of sins:

(1) The production and endless consumption of needless goods and services that are required in order to make their systems function.[1]

(2) The inducement of a constant state of hunger in consumers for a never-ending stream of new products, each of which promises to satisfy that hunger but never does; consumers are thus trapped in a suspended state of perpetual dissatisfaction and expectation.[2]

(3) The production of hazardous substances and materials which, when coupled with a callous disregard for human life and the environment, have proven extremely harmful both to individuals and to the environment as a whole.[3]

(4) The deepening intrusion of business into nearly every aspect of the culture and educational life of the nation so that business increasingly not only owns the means of production but the modes of expression and the places of exhibition of art and culture.[4]

What is of course so interesting about these charges is that with the exception of items 1 and 2 above, socialist societies are just as guilty of committing these very same sins. Without thereby letting Western societies and organizations off the hook, there is every reason to believe that many of the same sins would exist even if capitalism were suddenly to vanish from the face of the earth. For this reason alone, in a world that is increasingly dominated by business, it behooves us to examine the powerful effects that business organizations, East as well

1. Michael Parenti, *Inventing Reality, The Politics of the Mass Media*. New York: St. Martin's Press, 1986.
2. *Ibid*.
3. *Ibid*.
4. Herbert I. Schiller, *Culture, Inc., The Corporate Takeover of Public Expression*. New York: Oxford University Press, 1989.

as West, have on people no matter what the outward form of the ideological system in which they are embedded.

It is estimated that in the U.S., less than 20 percent of the work force is self-employed.[5] If we reverse this figure, it means that over 80 percent are employed by someone else, i.e., work in an organization that is the creation of and run by someone else. Although numerous studies exist of the behavior and effects of organizations on workers and their families, middle managers, and even top executives, very few studies have focused predominantly on how the very top members of organizations mistreat themselves.[6] Without attempting to minimize the pain and suffering of those less fortunate or excusing those at the top because of the greater power that they wield, it is all the more important to note that they are often just as trapped in a vicious system from which they cannot escape. The parallels with a dysfunctional family (e.g., families that have a seriously alcoholic member or one who engages in physical abuse or violence) are very strong. *No one escapes unscathed or emotionally unscarred from a dysfunctional or unhealthy family.*

As we noted earlier, in the course of our ongoing research in the area of crisis management (CM), we and our colleagues have interviewed over 350 high-level executives in over 120 organizations. The organizations span virtually every type of manufacturing and service industry as well as major government agencies. As a result, we have every reason to believe in the generality of our findings. In a word, healthy as well as unhealthy individuals get trapped into playing an endless variety of unhealthy games. While this is true even of so-called "healthy organizations," it is even truer of organizations that are "unhealthy or dysfunctional" to begin with. The games we have observed are a powerful embodiment of the general mindset or culture of the organizations in which our interviewees work. The games not only maintain the very system in which these people work but they keep the organization locked into a state from which it cannot develop further. What is especially interesting is their perverse, "Catch-22" aspects. In many cases, they are used as devices to protect the individuals from the very sickness of the system in which they find themselves. The

5. See Donald L. Kanter and Philip Mirvis, *The Cynical Americans, Living and Working in an Age of Discontent and Disillusion.* San Francisco: Jossey-Bass, 1989.
6. For one of the few works that do, see Michael Maccoby, *The Gamesman: Winning and Losing the Career Game.* New York: Bantam Books, 1976. However, Maccoby is limited in the number of games that he treats.

supreme irony is that the very games that are used for protection against the system not only help to maintain it but are themselves some of the most strongly characteristic features of the system itself. In other words, *playing games is itself a fundamental part of The Game, i.e., the system itself.*

A day is a long time. If we estimate, conservatively, that we work an average of 170 hours per month for eleven and a half months per year, then we spend about 120,000 minutes at work per year. If, for whatever reasons, one's deepest inner core has been bruised or wounded, then one needs to fill up this inordinate amount of time with tasks and experiences that provide one with a sense of "busy-ness," aliveness, control, self-importance, or, at the very least, with tasks and experiences that do not overly threaten one's inner sense of self. For this reason, organizational players have for a long time invented a number of ("Busy-ness") games that allow them to avoid confronting issues that are too threatening and at the same time allow them to experience the sensation of being "busy." The games are especially needed in those cases where an organization produces a number of products and services that the members know are especially useless or harmful. In this way, the games generate a measure of self-impor-tance, rightness, and power, as well as financial compensation. Most of all, the games are more often than not played by high-echelon em-ployees such as managers, professionals, and executives who have the power to define the rules of the game for themselves, or, at a mini-mum, the various environments in which the games will be played.

WHY WE WORK: TO DERIVE ANSWERS
TO LIFE'S BASIC QUESTIONS

When we are young, we start on our careers, chosen or otherwise, with great hopes. We begin a lifetime punctuated by days of work and all too brief weekends and holidays of rest, fun, and renewal of the spirit. For some of us—the lucky few—our work will be one of our greatest sources of happiness and creativity. For others, it will be the source of our greatest hell, dangerous both to our physical and mental health as well as that of our loved ones. Whether blessed or not, most of us who work will spend on average 120,000 minutes each year dreaming dreams, hoping hopes until our dreams and our hopes have been either realized or dealt a fatal blow. A twenty-nine-year-old stu-dent in one of the first author's MBA classes at USC put it this way:

"Most of my peers . . . have given up by the time they are only twenty-six; for them, the game is over; work is just something you do for eight hours a day; fun is what you get after work; but it's over; most know that by the age of twenty-six they won't make it in the corporation; they won't realize their dreams."

When asked why we work, for most people, although it's important, money does not score highest on the list. Most of us work not just because we need to survive economically, but because we need to fill up our time on earth with something worthwhile. We work for a sense of who and what we are, what we might be, what we hope and dream not only for ourselves but for our children as well.

Beneath the surface, just barely, lie all the basic questions of life, no matter what the activity. Through our work we get answers, however imperfect—indeed because they are imperfect—to the fundamental questions. In unhealthy organizations, both the questions and the answers themselves become perverted. In such organizations, even the strongest people are drawn into playing dangerous games, not always of their own choosing.[7] The games themselves thus constitute the answers to life's basic questions that even healthy individuals are forced to accept.

Although the number of games is limited ultimately only by the creativity of the human imagination, we have identified twenty major games that individuals in Crisis-Prone organizations play, according to the best estimates from our data, *seven times more* than their counterparts in Crisis-Prepared or healthy organizations. Even though there is extreme overlap between them, it soon became apparent that the games could be grouped into five major categories:

(1) Identity Games
(2) Control/Protection/Repair Games
(3) Perfection/Entitlement Games
(4) Image Games
(5) Energy/Aliveness Games

To gain a quick sense of what the various games are about, it is enough to list the basic questions or issues that each is attempting to answer. Figure 1 shows the detailed sets of questions that each of the

7. See Douglas LaBier, *Modern Madness, The Emotional Fallout of Success*. Menlo Park, CA: Addison-Wesley, 1986.

general categories address. Figure 2 shows not only the general categories of games but the detailed individual games that are associated with each of them. In many cases, a particular game is listed under more than one general category, showing that not only is the overlap between categories great but that the same game addresses multiple concerns or issues at the same time.

Under *Identity Games* the basic questions are:

— Who/What am I?
— Where do I begin/leave off from the profession (e.g., accounting, engineering, law, etc.) that constitutes the source of my education/livelihood?
— Where do I begin/leave off from the corporation in which I practice my profession?

Under *Control/Protection/Repair Games* the basic questions are:

— How strong/weak am I, do I feel?
— How big and powerful am I, do I feel?
— How can I protect myself from others/the organization?
— How much do I need to protect/repair myself from others/the organization?
— How much am I in control of myself/others/the environment?
— How strong/powerful is my magic?
— How much can I exploit others/the environment?
— How much do I need to exploit others, etc.?
— How much can I be exploited by others/the environment?
— What gives me power or a sense of it?
— What are the limits to my power/ability to affect things?
— How fragmented/disconnected versus integrated/connected am I, is the world around me?

Under *Perfection/Entitlement Games* the basic questions are:

— Am I basically good/worthy/deserving as a person?
— How much am I entitled to?
— How comfortable/accepting of myself and others am I?

— How nice/worthy/good do I have to be in order to be loved/accepted by others?

— How much can I exploit others? Whom can I exploit?

Under *Image Games* the questions are:

— Can I get by on image alone?

— Can I manipulate/control my image/career?

— Do I look good?

— Do I always have to look good?

— Can I get by with magic/illusions versus actual accomplishment?

Under *Energy/Aliveness Games* the questions are:

— How close can I skate to the razor's edge before I and those around me self-destruct?

— Do I basically feel alive in what I do?

— What makes me feel alive?

— What do I need to do in order to feel alive?

— How do I cope with boredom, hold it off? How do I cope with depression?

IDENTITY GAMES

1. The "Role Playing" or the "I-Am-My-Profession" Game

In Western societies especially, what a person *does* often defines who or what one *is*. The first game carries this notion to such an extreme that apart from the person's role, job, profession, etc., there is no person, or in the language of the preceding chapter, no "self" left over. In such cases, the person uses their role/job/profession to fill up a "self" that is literally empty or devoid of anything else that would round the person out and make them into a full human being.

This game is played especially when the structure of a person's "self" is defective to such a degree that the person is heavily dependent upon external factors, i.e., the opinions of others, the purchase of expensive cars, clothes, jewelry, the accumulation of fancy titles, homes, etc. This particular game is especially difficult to crack because of the ease with which it is started and maintained in American society, i.e., a society that is governed by a high degree of narcissism and specialization.

Extreme versions of this game are easily recognized by the nearly complete lack of spontaneity and/or absence of humor by the person playing it. If the game thus provides a high degree of comfort, orderliness, and structure in a world that increasingly is lacking in such virtues, it also constitutes a wall or a prison for the player as well. If there is extreme safety and comfort within the confines and structure that the game offers—and it does—then the game also serves to wall the person off from the feelings and considerations of other people and points of view.

Consequences of Game 1 for Crisis Management:

The Role Playing game leads to self-deception on the part of both individuals and organizations. In the area of CM, these can have disastrous consequences. For example, during our many interviews, we repeatedly encountered "financial experts" who defined something as a crisis "if and only if it had severe financial implications for *their* organization." This was their only concern. Completely absent was any concern for the environment, surrounding community, or the well-being of others. Similarly, we also repeatedly encountered public relations and public affairs executives who acknowledged crisis for them and their organization "if and only if it made the front page."

No profession was exempt from this line of reasoning. Every profession had its narrow advocates of what constituted a crisis for them and their organization. Thus, there were marketing executives for whom a crisis was nothing but a "severe drop in market share." In almost all cases, there is extreme confusion between the effects of a crisis and what constitutes crisis. No one denies, certainly least of all us, that a major crisis can produce a severe drop in market share and financial earnings, plus adverse publicity, etc.

The Role Playing game can also be disastrous in other ways. If there are major overt battles over power, as there inevitably are, then one of the most critical arenas in which this will be played out is in the area of CM. If one function or profession is viewed as dominant, then the danger is that its narrow, prescribed set of concerns will become the yardstick for dominating behavior during a major crisis. For instance, in many corporations the chief legal counsel is the head of the crisis team. This means that questions and concerns over legal liability will tend to predominate. Legal concerns will not only tend to dominate but have the effect of limiting information to the outside world. Thus, top corporate officials will be admonished against and in many cases prohibited from responding to natural inquiries and concerns from the public as well as the press. However, the head of public affairs will naturally point out that this is precisely one of the things that needs be done during a crisis. The point is not that neither of these two functions is entirely correct but that one needs to strike a proper balance. But what constitutes a "proper balance" is precisely one of the things that needs to be discussed thoroughly *before* a major crisis occurs. It is extremely difficult under any circumstances to work this out, least of all during the heat of an actual crisis.

Game Breakers:

We have also, thank God, encountered many who knew how to break this and all the other games. Many whom we interviewed understand the emptiness and the illusion of such games precisely because they have played them so well in the past. As a result, they have developed interests outside of work in order to grow so that they could be even more effective personally in life as well as in their chosen professions. If any one single thing stands out as a game *breaker*, it is the ability to see the utter ridiculousness of one's chosen profession and hence the ability to be able to laugh at it and oneself.

2. The MBA ("Me Before Anyone") or "Me, Me, Me" Game

Motivation:

This particular game is the clearest and strongest expression of the classic notion of narcissism: selfishness and self-centeredness. As we noted in the last chapter, those who most often are identified as narcissists do not in fact love themselves enough. Their sense of self-worth and self-esteem is precarious.

This game is often associated with dramatic behaviors that are on the edge of what are considered moral or legal. They are also reinforced by the excessive demands that organizations place on their top or key members for "dramatic" performance.

General Signs:

The "star" system of Wall Street, the scandals in business, politics, and religion associated with such names as Jim Bakker, Ivan Boesky, Charles Brown, Leona Helmsley, Michael Milliken, Oliver North, and Jim Wright are prime examples of this game. The American public often plays the role of a co-conspirator in both starting and maintaining this game. The public is generally fascinated not only by such acts themselves, but by the chutzpah of those who are bold enough to engage in and carry them out, as well as by the excessive publicity that they generate. There is little doubt that many who condemn them identify vicariously nonetheless with the acts as well as the players themselves. There is also very little doubt that the extreme publicity that is given to the very few who are associated with the most dramatic examples generates a false sense of security by allowing the American public to project the causes for the crises that are generated as a result of them onto the very few who perpetrate them. The true problem however lies much deeper. We need to focus not only on the specific cases that make the headlines but also on those of countless executives who play similar games as well. The difficulty is that the countless others who play these games do so in a much less dramatic fashion and are therefore much more difficult to discover and to correct.

Consequences for Crisis Management:

Those who are involved in the MBA game are only interested in CM if they judge that a crisis can potentially threaten their own narrow self-interest, or if they stand a chance to benefit, for example, emerge as a "white knight." One of the strongest motivations driving those who play the MBA game is the need to be perceived as "the savior of the world." In addition, they also play a subsidiary game, "I Need to Look Good." A prime example is Alexander Haig with his famous "I am in charge" statement in the aftermath of Watergate. This game is an extremely dangerous one to play in crisis situations because it often results in dramatic and grandiose moves that can actually harm or even destroy an organization more than it can help it.

CONTROL/PROTECTION/REPAIR GAMES

3. The "Fragmentation," "Compartmentalization," or "Splitting Reality" Game

Motivation:

This game is strongly related to the Role Playing game. The primary difference between the two is whereas the first game fragments or splits the world into a set of narrow, rigidly defined *professions*, this one splits the world into a set of narrow, rigid *distinctions*, e.g., "inside" versus "outside" the corporation. The primary purpose of these distinctions is to provide an illusion of mastery or control over one's inner world, what we have referred to as a person's deepest inner core or "self."

Those who play this game do so in order to live in their own artificially constructed "little world" where they can experience far less anxiety than if they had to deal with a complex reality that less and less fits into any preconceived set of categories. Also, as in the first game, this one is similarly reinforced by the increasing societal trend toward specialization.

General Signs and Consequences for Crisis Management:

Crisis-Prone organizations fragment their view of the world in four principle ways:

(1) Internal/external or "inside" the corporation factors versus "outside" the corporation factors; the major implication is that only what goes on inside is of direct relevance. In other words, a crisis is defined only in relation to its effects *on the organization* not on the surrounding community and environment.

(2) Economic/technical factors versus human/social factors or considerations; for example, Union Carbide made a series of decisions with regard to its Bhopal, India, plant that not only were based on financial considerations but lacked any explicit consideration of the impact of these decisions on the total system or surrounding environment. Because the market for pesticides had dropped pre-

cipitously, Union Carbide made the decision to cut further additional investment in the Bhopal plant. The result
was a number of key personnel being let go. This in turn
had the effect of lowering the morale of those who remained. In addition, those who stayed had less experience in operating the plant. The consequence was that a
series of decisions designed primarily to treat a "financial crisis" contribued significantly to human operator
error resulting in the catastrophic release of deadly gas.
There are numerous other examples of this type where an
action taken in one area (e.g., technical) leads to catas-
tropic consequences in another area (e.g., human). This
is the basis for the strong statement that we made in
Chapter 1 where we contended that rarely, if ever, is the
final end link in a chain solely responsible for the occurrence of a major crisis. Rather, a crisis is typically the
result of a whole series of actions or inactions that originate from the major structure or culture of the
organization.

(3) The extreme splitting or dichotomization of stakeholder
parties into important versus unimportant groups; in general, executives in Crisis-Prone organizations only consider a very limited class of stakeholders or parties that
can affect their organization, typically only those who
wield significant power. Thus, in the case of Exxon,
plants and animals were not considered as important
"stakeholders," and in the case of Bhopal, neither Union
Carbide nor the Indian government considered the thousands of poor people who had crowded up immediately
around the plant as "significant" stakeholders. Indeed,
the victims in the vicinity of the plant were living, literally, under the illusion that the factory produced "medi-
cine for plants or vegetation."

(4) Extreme splitting of the properties of stakeholders themselves; Crisis-Prone organizations tend to view others, if
they even view them at all, only as "customers," "government regulators," "competitors," "unions," etc., and
not as "fellow human beings." In this way, Crisis-Prone
organizations are able to view outsiders as impersonal

"entities" to be exploited, neutralized, overcome, bought off, etc.

Game Breakers:

Managers in Crisis-Prepared organizations engage in fragmentation to a far less degree. In addition, they hold a much more systemic view of the world. They have developed a number of mechanisms for integrating different perspectives within their organization and themselves. In general, they not only operate from a variety of professional perspectives, but they understand fundamentally the necessity for both viewing and treating human beings in their "full complexity."

4. The "Buffering," "Drawbridge," "Perpetual Inaction Machine," or "Status Quo" Game

Deep Motivation:

The motivation behind this game is the basic desire to protect the person's current sense of "self" through a strong refusal to change. Those who play this game not only are attached rigidly to their personal life experiences, if not personal history, but, as a result, are unable to incorporate new experiences into their existing sense of "self." To put it mildly, the game is reinforced by all of the innumerable mechanisms in organizations and society that defend the status quo.

General Signs:

The Buffering game is one of the oldest played in organizations. As such, it is widely recognized and practiced. Its tactics are multiple: canceling appointments at the last minute and constantly rescheduling them months in advance; forming a task force or committee on a project whose findings will then be delayed and/or sabotaged; placing an incompetent at the head of a project one wants to see fail; providing insufficient resources to a project; fomenting any one of a number of malicious rumors; giving one's verbal support to an important project, but not acting on it; producing voluminous numbers of highly technical reports that no one will read; etc.

Consequences for Crisis Management:

While some buffering strategies are obviously necessary in all organizations in order that they can focus on those things that are truly important, some of the tactics associated wtih this game have consequences that are absolutely disastrous. For example, the health problems associated with the handling and production of asbestos were known scientifically and medically as early as 1910. However, buffering strategies by companies such as Johns-Manville delayed action until the mid-1970s, thus resulting in the deaths of additional thousands of employees. For another, threats to the ozone layer have been known scientifically since the early 1960s, but the issue was only starting to be acknowledged at the end of the 1980s.

One of the most important tactics used by executives in Crisis-Prone organizations is the commissioning of different scientific studies for the express purpose of "disproving" the scientific findings advanced by others who threaten the corporate mission of their organization. For instance, scientific battles have played a major role in the Bhopal disaster. The variation on the number of deaths reported and/or estimated still ranges between 1,600 and 10,000.[8] For another, the exact nature of the gas that was released, the presence of cyanide—a very toxic gas used during wartime—has been strongly "confirmed" by some and just as hotly denied by others. Similarly, the nature of the long-term effect of the injuries has ranged between no effects to long term and even inter-generational. When a major crisis happens, those external stakeholders who especially feel that they have been "buffered out of existence"—i.e., not told the full truth prior to the crisis— tend to retaliate strongly against the corporation, as demonstrated by the lawsuits against Union Carbide by its shareholders for "basic misrepresentation of the dangers involved in operating the plant."

Game Breakers:

Executives in Crisis-Prepared organizations also use a number of buffering strategies in order to keep proper focus while in their jobs. But they also have the commitment to contend with a threatening issue in its early stages. They understand that there are no magic solutions

---

8. Paul Shrivastava, *Bhopal, Anatomy of a Crisis*. Cambridge, MA: Ballinger Publishing Company, 1987.

to complex problems. To manage an issue in its early developmental phases is not only much easier but also may very likely decrease the chance of "snowballing" effects later.

5. The "Blaming" Game

Deep Motivation:

The Blaming game is closely associated with the previous one. However, the crucial point is that it is played *after* a major disaster has occurred rather than *prior to* it. Its primary function is to deny responsibility for a disaster and to convince both oneself and others that one does not need to change at all. Its fundamental function is to maintain the status quo indefinitely.

General Signs:

To an extent, many Buffering games end up as Blaming games. When this happens, one has the opportunity to witness a perverse form of reasoning or logic. Executives in Crisis-Prone organizations blame their *prior* failure to handle a major crisis—head it off, prepare for it, etc.—on the crisis itself! That is, they fundamentaly reverse cause and effect. The occurrence of the crisis, the effect of a prior Buffering game, becomes the cause or the rationalization for their previous failure to act! They do this through the use of such linguistic ploys as "the problem was too big to be handled quickly." Through the use of such devices, they fail to acknowledge that it was precisely *their previous playing* of the Buffering game that contributed significantly not only to the disaster itself but to its magnitude. Exxon Valdez is merely the latest example of this game.

Consequences for Crisis Management

The effects of Blaming games are extremely visible in post-crises remedies. They basically set the stage for how similar crises will be handled in the future. Their primary purpose is to diminish the effects and the importance of some of the most powerful issues that could threaten the status quo. For example, Union Carbide's blaming of the Bhopal disaster on "sabotage"[9] not only has had the effect of decreas-

9. *Ibid.*

ing the amount of financial compensation that was paid to the real victims, but it also diverted the discussion of the responsibility of First World corporations operating in Third World countries. To some extent, the use of the Blaming game by Union Carbide has also helped to maintain other games that we will be discussing such as the "Resourcism" game, which is also played in the Third World. It has also helped to maintain the "I Should Always Look Good" game for Union Carbide's top management. In this way, Union Carbide's top executives can perceive themselves as the "victims," thereby reducing their own guilt and responsibility. For another, Exxon's blaming of the Valdez accident on one man acted both to diminish the overall responsibility of Exxon as a company and to divert attention from such threatening questions as the virtual impossibility of operating large oil tankers at sea in complete safety.

The Blaming game also helps to maintain other games such as "Bigger Is Better" by blaming the disaster not on the fundamental type of technology used—giant tankers which by their very nature are almost bound to cause a major accident—but solely on human error. The technologies involved are given absolution, therefore reinforcing what we describe later as the "Technophilia" game. It is perhaps self-evident that the Blaming game is but another expession of the Fragmentation game in that it does not acknowledge that human factors are an integral part of the operation of all technical systems, and vice versa. The point is that technical and human factors are so intertwined that they are inseparable.

Game Breakers:

Those executives in Crisis-Prepared organizations that we have interviewed have a far greater capacity for recognizing as well as acknowledging their responsibilities and their mistakes. For example, Johnson & Johnson realized the impossibility, from a technical perspective, of completely protecting Tylenol from being tampered with in its then-current package design. As a result, J&J modified the design of their product at the overall cost of some $200 million.

6. The "Get Even" Game

Deep Motivation:

This game is played when a person's deepest sense of "self" has been injured by another. It is important to understand that it does not matter at all if the "felt injury" is actually due to another person. What matters only is that an individual with a problematic sense of self perceives that another is responsible for the injury.

In extreme cases, the entire world is blamed. In such cases, the motivation is to get even with society. One of the most prominent examples is Shakespeare's Richard III, who believed that he had the right to commit evil because nature itself was at fault for having cheated him through his physical handicaps.

General Signs:

The increasing prominence of lawyers in the U.S. is perhaps the clearest indication of the importance of the "Get Even" game. As such, lawyers function both to protect the organization against the Get Even games of others as well as to allow their own organizations to play Get Even themselves. Currently the U.S. has a total of some 600,000 lawyers, or one for every 400 citizens, while Japan has about one lawyer for every 10,000.

Another sign of the importance and vitality of this game can be seen in corporate theft and criminality. In a recent survey[10] conducted in large organizations, one-third of the employees admitted to having stolen some company property. The total cost of employee theft is estimated at between some $5 billion and $10 billion a year.[11] It should be stressed that most of the employees surveyed expressed a deep dissatisfaction with their employers and thus appeared to be playing Get Even through their criminal behavior. In addition, almost two-thirds of the same employees reported other types of sabotage, such as frequent abuse of sick leave, long lunch and coffee breaks, falsification of time

10. See J. P. Clark and R. C. Hollinger, "Theft by Employees in Work Organizations," Washington, DC: U.S. Department of Justice, 1983. See also Donald L. Kanter and Philip H. Mirvis, *The Cynical Americans, Living and Working in an Age of Discontent and Disillusion.* San Francisco: Jossey-Bass, 1989.
11. See R. Bartol and A. M. Bartol, *Criminal Behavior, A Psychological Approach.* Englewood Cliffs, NJ: Prentice Hall, 1986, pp. 256-265. See also Donald L. Kanter and Philip H. Mirvis, *op. cit.*

sheets, as well as slow and sloppy workmanship.

Consequences for Crisis Management:

Buffering, Blaming, and Get Even games all have a very strong potential for lawsuits and their attendant consequences, such as high costs. They also have the potential for creating further crises. For example, the Illinois Bell Telephone Company (IBT) has recently been blamed, by some of its major stakeholders, as being solely responsible for the recent telecommunications outage that affected the entire Chicago area. As a result, IBT has been sued for hundreds of millions of dollars. In other words, some of IBT's principal stakeholders have played the Get Even game with a vengeance.

Get Even games inside of organizations, such as sabotage, can be especially dangerous considering the tight coupling or strong interactions that now exist between virtually all complex technologies. It is currently estimated that high-tech thieves collect somewhere between $3 billion and $5 billion a year from U.S. companies and that nearly 40 percent of the *Fortune* 500 companies have been affected by "computer viruses," thus leading to interference with the normal operation of information systems.[12] This threat is neither minor nor inconsequential when you realize that at present some 85 percent of the *Fortune* 500 firms are now totally dependent on their information technologies for their day-to-day operations, and hence, sheer survival.

Game Breakers:

Those executives that we have interviewed in Crisis-Prepared organizations engage far less in Get Even games. Their initial sense of being wounded is far less than that of executives in Crisis-Prone organizations. This is not to say that they do not and will not engage in legal battles if they are necessary. However, they understand much more fully Gandhi's acute observation that to "exact an eye for an eye has the ultimate consequence of making the entire world blind." Executives in Crisis-Prepared organizations exhibit to a much lesser degree the tendency to view their employees as merely "human resources," and the far greater tendency to view them as total human beings. As a result, they experience problems of sabotage and tampering far less

12. Paul Tate, "Risk! The Third Factor," *Datamation*, April 15, 1988.

and sustain a far greater commitment from their employees to the organization. In response they have developed entirely different CM
procedures and processes for protecting themselves and others.

7. The "Be Nice to People" Game

Deep Motivation:

It is tempting to view this game as the complete reverse of the Get
Even game. However, no one should be fooled at all by its surface
harmlessness. Because it seems so benign, it can be every bit as devastating as the Get Even game.

The motivation for this game springs basically from the incapacity
of many individuals to tolerate and to sustain conflict. The structure of
what we have called the "self" of many people requires so much
understanding and admiration from others that they are deeply afraid
of and resistant to direct confrontation. This game is often reinforced
by the advice of many organizational development consultants who
preach, wrongly, that an organization needs to be free of conflict in
order to function. *This view is totally erroneous!* Healthy individuals
like healthy families and organizations are not free of all conflict but
rather have developed the ability and the capacity to make productive
use of conflict.

General Signs:

The present inability of many managers to confront others is overwhelming. For example, a recent survey of more than 4,000 executives in *Fortune* 500 companies revealed that five executives out of
seven preferred to lie to their employees about their poor performance
rather than confront them directly.[13] To some extent, this particular
game can be seen as another version of the Buffering game when issues that need confrontation are not addressed explicitly. An extreme
case was played at Ford prior to Iacocca's departure. As noted in his
biography,[14] Iacocca was never told directly that he needed to go, but
for three long years before his departure, his power was continually

---

13. J. Halper, *Quiet Desperation, The Truth About Successful Men.* New York: Warner Books,
   1988. Kanter and Mirvis, *op. cit.*
14. D. Abodaher, *Iacocca, America's Most Dynamic Businessman!* New York: Kensington Publishing Company, 1982.

undermined and he was no longer invited to participate in important strategic decisions. To some extent, it also seems that Iacocca had also "fooled himself" into believing that he would take Ford's place.

Consequences for Crisis Management:

This game reinforces the "I Should Always Look Good" game as well as diminishes the possibility for an organization to develop a true culture of whistle-blowing with regard to potential crises. In essence, it forbids managers to tell one another the truth and thereby realistically assess the potential for future crises. It seems that this game was particularly active in NASA prior to the Challenger disaster.[15] This particular game also has a number of major implications for organizational politics that we will discuss in the "Buddies" game.

Game Breakers:

Executives in Crisis-Prepared organizations do not confuse empathy with sympathy. They understand well that to respect someone it is not necessary to always agree with that person. Also, they understand the positive sides of conflict. Conflict is not used against a particular person but is used in order to reinforce the healthy functioning of a group or the growth of people. The existence of conflict is not used as an excuse to engage in blaming people but instead to locate the true sources of problems and to work on them.

8. The "Buddies" Game

Deep Motivation:

This game is also one of the oldest played in organizations. It is motivated by intense fear and anxiety. When threatened, those who have deep flaws in their basic sense of self have a tendency to form coalitions and clans in order to protect not only their basic sense of "rightness" but their basic sense of who and what they are. This game is reinforced by the tremendous group and economic pressures that

---

15. Report of the President's Commission on the Space Shuttle Challenger Accident, Order No. 04000000496-3, GPO Superintendent of Documents, Government Printing Office, Washington, DC 20402-9325.

exist in most organizations. One is either a "member of the *team* or not."

General Signs:

In many, if not most organizations, political maneuvering is especially strong. The exercise of power and the strength of coalitions formed between various individuals and departments allow for the possibility of making relatively rapid decisions and implementing quick actions. However, political games or, as we call them, Buddies games can be destructive when they are played out of deep feelings of insecurity.

A number of prominent critics have denounced the political battles that often exist, particularly between staff and line. Abraham Zaleznik, for example, has traced many of these battles to the management principles first proposed by Alfred Sloan, one of the earliest CEOs of General Motors and whose principles still form the basis of how many large organizations are managed today.[16] Zaleznik attributes the present separation between strategy and finance at the corporate staff level and operations at the line level to Sloan's deep incapacity to confront issues. Or what we call the Be Nice to People game. Often, the Buddies games that result from such structural separations end up in destructive battles between line and corporate staff over issues of power.

Consequences for Crisis Management:

One of the most negative impacts of this game with regard to CM is the development of a chronic mistrust between staff and line people. Often line managers blame their corporate staff for not understanding the details of their day-to-day operations. At the same time, line managers often accuse those at the corporate level of wanting to have total power over line operations. For its part, corporate holds line executives directly responsible for the day-to-day management of operations. Caught between these conflicting pressures, line managers and executives try to minimize, as best they can, the power base of corporate staff and to effectively run their own operations.

16. Abraham Zaleznik, "Power and Politics in Organizational LIfe," *Harvard Business Review*, Vol. 48, pp. 47-60, 1975; Abraham Zaleznik and M. Kets de Vries, *Power and the Corporate Mind*. Boston, MA: Houghton, Mifflin & Co., 1975.

We have seen this game many times in Crisis-Prone organizations—to put it mildly. The game requires that line managers give an impression that they are "open" to the scrutiny of their corporate staff. They encourage the staff to focus exclusively on the success of their targeted budgets in an attempt to keep them away from operations as much as possible. One line manager in an oil company stressed, "If I screw up the budgets, *they* will come over here and run my business." In this statement you can recognize the similarities between this game and some of the others previously discussed, i.e, the Fragmentation game. In this case, the fragmentation exists between line and staff. Other games, such as Buffering, were also in operation in that both parties attempted to shy away from confronting real issues. One of the major costs of the Buddies game is that corporate employees as a whole will not be aware of potentially threatening issues in the company's operations. And further, line managers may be tempted to take a number of risky courses of action in order to meet their targeted budgets at all costs.

Game Breakers:

Executives in Crisis-Prepared companies know how to minimize such games by simultaneously reducing the overall power of their corporate staff and increasing responsibilities at the line operational levels. They do this by establishing close cooperation, trust, and communication between executives at all levels. They understand that CM needs to be done both at the operating line level and at the corporate staff level. They realize that in the critical area of CM it is not an "either/or," but rather a "both/and."

9. The "Cocoon" Game

Deep Motivation:

This game is motivated primarily by a retreat of the self to a safe, familiar haven where it both can be protected and can recover from the overwhelming threats that are perceived in the outside world. The Cocoon game is played in order to escape the reality of the threats altogether. It is also played in order to "take care of oneself," to stay put in the present by separating oneself from the rest of the community.

General Signs:

Cocooners, as trend observers call them, are likely to retreat during the weekend to the isolation of their own homes in order to recuperate from all the Role Playing games they have been forced to engage in during the week. One Cocooner to whom we spoke put it as follows: "I don't want to talk to anyone. I don't want to smile. Going out means constantly having to perform. After a week of performances, you want a day off." It is thus no surprise to find that a great number of products are now offered on the market that respond precisely to the needs of Cocooners: high-quality stereo and home video systems; a wide range of home delivery services, including food, clothing, furniture, etc.

Consequences for Crisis Management:

The net effect of the Cocoon game for CM is noncommitment or noninvolvement. To a certain extent, this game is reminiscent of the MBA or Me Before Anyone game. However, while the MBA game engages the individual *in fighting against the world*, the Cocoon game is much more of a *retreat from* the world. Some individuals manage to combine both, to wit, the quote given in the previous paragraph. The Cocoon game dictates that executives in Crisis-Prone organizations not engage in issues that are not considered to be "directly in their own backyard." For example, an executive in an international food and restaurant company stated that terrorist activities in his company's foreign divisions were *their* problems.

Game Breakers:

Executives in Crisis-Prepared organizations also use cocooning to a certain extent. They may also retreat to their homes and havens to recuperate when threatened and beaten down. Indeed, all of us do from time to time. For this very reason, many Crisis-Prepared organizations have explicitly developed "company-wide cocoons" for their employees. However, these executives do not use cocoons as a retreat for *denying* the reality of the external world. They use them more as valves for letting off steam. Thus, they are not playing the Cocoon game in response to the cycle of being on and off stage, spending a terrifying time in the "jungle out there," and then coming back to their "cocoon." Rather, their actions are much more evenly focused on the day-to-day tasks at hand. These executives have also developed the capacity to dream about the future and to engage in actions that actually can bring about a better world. They are actively involved in steps to make their visions come true.

10. The "Technophilia" Game

Deep Motivation:

This game is a very close relation to an important one that we will encounter later, the "Magician's" game. Like the Magician's game, the Technophilia game is also associated with strong feelings of omnipotence and invulnerability. This particular game is especially reinforced by the extremely strong belief in American society that bigger and better technology can, in principle, solve all our problems. Even in response to the problems created by technology, the answer is always "to throw more technology at the problem."

General Signs:

The importance of this particular game is perhaps best demonstrated by a recent cover story in *Fortune* announcing "The Big Cleanup of Environmental Damage."[17] The article unfortunately does not take into account the seriousness of the situation, such as the fact that more than 15 percent of the U.S.'s soil for agriculture is now biologically dead. The article inappropriately uses the metaphor of a house where one can supposedly "stop time" for a while, "clean up one's mess," and then continue on as if everything was merely "business as usual." Another powerful example is the promise offered by the latest information technologies for resolving two of the most important issues that all organizations confront: the increased complexity of all problems and the need to produce even quicker solutions to them. Technology is now so deeply embedded into every level of our society that it has become almost invisible. It only becomes visible when our dependency on it is dramatically exposed, as in the case of the Illinois Bell crisis mentioned earlier. In the case of the breakdown

---

17. Anonymous, "Here Comes the Big New Cleanup," *Fortune*, November 21, 1988, pp. 102-18.

of telecommunications in Chicago, many of the people whom we interviewed in those firms commented that "it made us aware of the telephone all over again; before the crisis, the telephone was just something that we all took for granted."

Consequences for Crisis Management:

We have already touched on the important issue of the tight coupling that now exists between virtually all complex technologies, such that a breakdown in any one of them is enough to set off a chain reaction resulting in the breakdown in virtually all other technologies. The Technophilia game often makes problems even worse than they were before. Technologically based solutions often create new problems in their wake. For example, the use of radar technology in commercial marine vessels triggered a significant increase in accidents soon after it was introduced.[18] Because of the new technology, skippers thought that they could pilot their boats even faster without having to be more careful. In addition, more and more organizations are discovering that they are highly dependent on information technologies. This means that with the development of new crises such as computer viruses, bigger breakdowns in computer systems, or out and out sabotage, they are more vulnerable to disruptions than ever before. In essence, many organizations have become hostage to their new technologies. At present, it is believed that most major financial institutions could survive only for a few days after an interruption to their information technologies. In the medical sciences, this is known as the "iatrogenic effect." One finds that the patient is often left in worse condition after being treated by a technique that was supposed to make them better.

Game Breakers:

Executives in Crisis-Prepared organizations are much more critical about the introduction and use of technology. Before any technology is introduced, its potential negative effects are evaluated. One insurance company recognized that it was dangerous to merely "throw hardware at critical problems." Other firms that we have studied are busily engaged in "de-automation" in certain areas recognizing that

18. Charles Perrow, *Normal Accidents*. New York: Basic Books, 1984.

their dependency on advanced information technology is dangerous. The point is not that these firms are thereby rejecting and throwing all their technology out in some Luddite reaction. Rather, they have adopted a much more critical stance toward the acceptance of technology per se.

Chapter 4

Crisis Games II

They are playing a game. They are playing at not playing a game. If I show them I see they are, I shall break the rules and they will punish me. I must play their game, of not seeing I see the game.

R.D. Laing, *Knots*,
Pantheon, 1970

The human equivalent of commodity fetishism is the cult of the celebrity, which might be called a kind of image fetishism. Just as advertising transforms products into desirable images, celebrity image-managers transform human beings into icons of desire. Celebrities are people with attractive surfaces, images that play to the cameras. They are like mirrors, reflecting back the dreams and desires of those who worship them. Whatever human reality lurks behind the image, whatever doesn't show up on camera is irrelevant. In fact, in the post-modern age, one often gets the impression that there *is* nothing behind the image.

In the age of the Cross and the Virgin, one did not speak of one's "image." Rather, human beings were thought of as creatures with souls, or spirits, or characters that were fixed at birth. But in an age where the Dynamo has lent its electric energy to TV, human beings are being redefined. Today we think of ourselves as actors, as role players who can wear many different social masks, adopt any number of "looks" or images. Like TV heroes, we can change our roles by rewriting our own scripts, become someone else, exchange one image for another. Mask yields to mask.

Jack Solomon,
The Signs of Our Times,
Los Angeles: Jeremy Tarcher,
1988, p. 226

ENERGY/ALIVENESS GAMES

11. The "Razor's Edge" Game

Deep Motivation:

This game is played particularly in relation to painful if not chronic feelings of boredom. Its function is to allow individuals literally to "feel alive" for brief periods of time. It is reinforced by innumerable group, cultural, and social factors that pressure individuals into "macho" game behaviors.

General Signs and Consequences for Crisis Management:

Perhaps the clearest example of the relation between this game and CM is exemplified by the crisis if not failure of the giant brokerage firm E.F. Hutton. This game was associated with E.F. Hutton's aggressive cash management strategy and its risky ventures outside the law.

During our many interviews, we have met scores of individuals who could literally drive any corporate director of security "nuts." A number of workers in electric power companies refused to work on repairing electric lines if the power, some 15,000 kilowatts, was not "on." The reason is that the job was too "boring" if the power was shut off, as the safety regulations of the company required. Others that we have interviewed in nuclear facilities refused to wear safety protection gear arguing they had developed a "personal immune system" against nuclear radiation. Some computer programmers "get off" on building the most complicated programs possible so that they are constantly on the edge of "losing it." They relish constructing a program so big so that no one, including themselves, can fully understand what they have built. They also relish the experience of building a program so complex that an inadvertent move or error would "wipe out all of their efforts."

These examples are perhaps the clearest demonstration of the differences between the traditional "rational" views of human behavior and existential ones. In a real sense, executives in Crisis-Prone organizations *need* to take tremendous risks in order to "feel alive," although from a "rational standpoint" their behavior is totally irrational. We have also encountered numerous executives in the financial industry who were explicitly "managing by crises" through their development of a number of highly risky strategies "merely for the thrill of it." Such strategies go far beyond the traditional economic motives of increased financial return. *For such individuals, CM itself constitutes a "crisis" because it reduces the possibility of playing the Razor's Edge game!*

As a result, we need to question seriously whether the so-called present concern for CM, as small as it still is, is nonetheless connected in some strange way to the deep sense of boredom that inhabits far too many organizations. The present interest in CM is somewhat similar to the situation in the 1960s where a desire for "dramatic management" was developed in the U.S. government, especially as typified by President Nixon's management style.

Game Breakers:

While even executives in Crisis-Prepared organizations take risks and enjoy the thrills that are derived from them, they can still differentiate between their personal need for excitement and the potential dangers. In other words, they try to threaten the safety of others out of their own needs.

12. The "Apathy" or "Numbing Out" Game

Deep Motivation:

It is sad but true that many of us do not want to feel anything because to do so would require us to confront the emptiness of our lives. This particular game allows people to survive emotionally by not confronting themselves. Unfortunately, it also leads to being cut off from others. One cannot make emotional contact with others if one has not first made emotional contact with oneself.

General Signs:

Richard Sennet has argued that the most preponderant form of authority in organizations today is precisely that of "authority without love," i.e., dispassionate authority that is based only on utilitarian principles.[1] As we will see shortly, the relation of this game to that which we call "Resourcism" is very strong. In both cases, people are treated as resources whose only function is to be used, consumed, thrown out, and ultimately replaced by someone else.

The Apathy game is widely played in many organizations. Many marketing departments collect reams of "cold" data that are far removed from the real needs of their customers. This data is derived primarily from questionnaires and surveys as opposed to meeting customers directly.

Professionals are constantly being reprimanded to act as "true professionals," thereby enjoined from exhibiting real human emotions such as anger, frustration, or pain. In this way, other games such as the Role Playing game are also reinforced. In many ways, it can be contended that one of the techniques advocated by Peters and Waterman in their best-selling book *In Search of Excellence*,[2] i.e., "Management by Walking Around," is merely a superficial attempt to make up for the fact that human relations are poor at best in far too many organizations.

Consequences for Crisis Management:

During our many interviews, especially with managers in Crisis-Prone organizations, many executives themselves announced in one way or another that they were playing the Apathy game. For example, an executive at a major airline stated, "In this company, top management does not allow us to be stressed out; we have to be 'macho' enough to take it." Similarly an executive in a large retail organization said, "In this company, you cannot go to a seminar if the word 'stress' is in the title."

1. Richard Sennet, *Authority*. New York: Random House, 1980.
2. Tom Peters and R. H. Waterman, *In Search of Excellence, Lessons From America's Best Run Companies*. New York: Harper & Row, 1982.

We have also witnessed the influence of "hard cold data" in the area of CM. For example, the director of public relations in a large telecommunications firm that experienced a major crisis chose, as we emphasized earlier, to learn on TV of the reaction of the firm's customers as opposed to visiting and speaking directly with them. In another case, a marketing executive in a large fruit company stated that he did not have the time to listen to the thirty-minute audiotapes his customer complaint department was sending him every month, arguing that the sampling was not "scientifically representative of the total situation."

Game Breakers:

Executives in Crisis-Prepared organizations recognize the importance of integrating both thinking and feeling and have initiated a number of programs to promote such integration. For example, one engineer in a Crisis-Prepared organization, after the near crash of one of its airplanes, explicitly let the pilot of the airplane talk for two hours to the hundreds of employees who had worked on the plane, telling them how "he felt up there" when he lost control of the plane due to a technical failure. It is especially important to note that the pilot's talk was not intended to blame the employees in any way, but rather, to have all of them become more sensitive to the complexities of the technology and processes on which they were all working. Other firms have started a number of stress management programs or even developed diverse wellness programs focusing on both the physical and emotional health of their employees. We have heard over and over again how such programs have not only had positive effects on how a firm's internal employees feel about themselves, but have spilled over to relationships with customers on the outside. *One cannot attend to the concerns and issues of those outside the firm unless those on the inside have first listened and attended seriously to their own emotional concerns.*

13. The "Poor Me" or "Victims" Game

Deep Motivation:

This game is motivated by an overwhelming sense of being "crushed" by the world without any hope for betterment in the future.

This game is different from the Me Before Anyone Else game where the individual is fighting for himself and the Cocoon game where the individual is protecting himself. Rather, the Poor Me game is played by individuals who have developed a deep internal sense that they have "lost," that they are not "good enough," and further, that their deepest feelings, mainly defects, are going to be discovered by others.

General Signs:

One of the great dangers of this game is that it pushes people to admire and to follow the most dramatic, visible characters in society in order to feel a tremendous sense of power, strength, and omnipotence through their association with them. This was indeed what was felt by a large number of Germans during the rise of Hitler. And they literally made him into a "god." To a lesser degree, the American public played a similar game with Ronald Reagan. As we stressed in the previous chapter, it seems that a large number of people idealize corporate leaders who project an image of strength and power. The biographer of James Goldsmith may have captured this best when he wrote "Goldsmith . . . lives out the fantasies of others with a flamboyance that is unmistakable."[3]

Consequences for Crisis Management:

One of the worst consequences of this game is that it allows and even amplifies so many of the crisis or "Busy-ness games" that we have presented in this and the preceding chapter. Executives in Crisis-Prone organizations especially attempt to imitate the idealized leader or leaders who play these games. In essence, the Poor Me game reinforces the status quo of game playing as opposed to focusing on the substantive business at hand. The employees of Michael Milliken, for example, describe their hero as "a god with whom everything was possible." This is similar to the statement made by one of our respondents in a large oil company who said, "Our CEO can handle anything." Often, the Poor Me or Victims game leads many executives to invoke fate as the cause for most crises. Such executives also tend to stress their overall incapacity in managing anything and as a result refuse any involvement in CM as well. Lastly, this game also leads

3. G. Wansell, *Tycoon, the Life of James Goldsmith*. New York: Atheneum, 1987, p. 11.

executives in Crisis-Prone organizations to unwittingly sabotage themselves. Their deep fear that others will sooner or later discover their "deep inadequacies" strangely enough confirms their own inadequacies.

Game Breakers:

Executives in Crisis-Prepared organizations neither are "crushed" by the world, having formed a healthy sense of their own self-worth and competency, nor have they developed an inflated sense of themselves denying the existence of threats altogether. Echoing Kierkegaard, executives in Crisis-Prepared organizations have "learned rightly to be anxious."

PERFECTION/ENTITLEMENT GAMES

14. The "Search for Excellence" or "We Must Be Perfect" Game

Deep Motivation:

This game provides a powerful sense of feeling alive and worthwhile. This dual focus is perhaps the reason why it is played so much.

General Signs:

This game was typified by *In Search of Excellence* by Peters and Waterman in 1982.[4] The book stayed on *The New York Times* bestseller list for months, its total sales eventually reaching some 1.2 million copies.

Consequences for Crisis Management:

If the Search for Excellence can have positive effects on corporate behavior in general and on CM in particular, then it can also lead to corporate arrogance and smugness. For example, the feeling that "We're so good that everyone ought to love us and leave us alone." In this sense, the game then becomes more of a problem than part of the solution. During the course of our many interviews, we have repeatedly encountered a number of executives in Crisis-Prone organizations

---

4. Peters and Waterman, *op. cit.*

who did not believe that CM applied to them because they were "so excellent." For them, the Search for Excellence provided a strong rationalization for *not* engaging in CM.

One is puzzled by the definition of excellence that is given by many executives in Crisis-Prone organizations. Most of them define excellence as being a leader in their industry in total market share. Excellence is thus given as an excuse for playing the Bigger is Better game. Crisis-Prone organizations especially have the tendency to confuse "quality and substance." While a "junk" product could indeed be produced well, this does not change the basic fact that the product is still "junk." This is not to say that by winning at a "rat race," one is thereby made into a rat. The point is that executives in Crisis-Prone organizations basically do not understand that their employees cannot be motivated through the production of "junk" products. The field of marketing may be most at fault when it attempts to sell products through "gimmicks" rather than through true innovations. There currently exist more than fifty different flavors or varieties of dog food on the market. Similarly, there exist on the market more than 5,000 medicinal products, of which the World Health Organization has estimated only 50 are truly necessary. While a choice of color, taste, or packaging is important in democratic societies, the craze for market segmentation and "gimmicky products" not only pollutes our sense of values but in addition drives those who produce them to disinterest, thereby increasing the likelihood of crises. Finally, the Search for Excellence has engendered in many organizations the phenomenon of idealizing certain "star players" who are very adept at playing the I Should Always Look Good game.

Game Breakers:

Executives in Crisis-Prepared organizations fundamentally understand that the Search for Excellence cannot be measured solely in terms of market share, but rather, that excellence is the perpetual challenge to focus continually on the production of substantive products and services. Further, such executives do not believe in the magic curative powers of "excellence and perfection." Instead, they focus on being "good without perfection," realizing that the desire for perfection can be pathological. For example, one company we know of has stopped production of deodorizing aerosols because they did not truly treat "body odors," but rather dealt only with its symptoms and because the product contributed to the pollution of the environment. Most of all, Crisis-Prepared organizations know fundamentally that excellence is not a static end state or condition that once attained is attained forevermore. Instead, the Search for Excellence is a Continual Quest for Excellence.

15. The "Resourcism," "Entitlement" or "I Deserve All That I Can Get" Game

Deep Motivation:

This game derives from the powerful feeling that many in our society have that they are basically entitled to whatever they need and want. The game functions because whatever is outside of the person is viewed as a legitimate resource for filling up the person's inner felt sense of emptiness. As such, the game is strongly related to the Me Before Anyone Else and Fragmentation games.

General Signs:

Some of the most negative signs of the Resourcism game have been observed with regard to the environment. They are associated with issues such as global warming, the depletion of the ozone layer, the deforestation of many parts of the world, or the significant rise of toxic waste and the problems related to their disposal. There are so many more issues that are not discussed at the present time, such as the "death" of Lake Erie, the near death of the Rhine in Europe, the biological death of an estimated 15 percent of the agricultural lands in America, the fact that more than eleven million hectares turn into worthless desert every year, and so on. While the media do emphasize such problems, we do not hear as much about issues which operate at the level of society as a whole, such as the significant increase in the rates of suicide, criminality, consumption of drugs, as well as a dramatic increase in narcissistic behavior throughout society.

A recent issue of *Fortune* points out one of the latest versions of the Resourcism game, especially as it pertains to CEOs.[5] It seems that

5. Julie Connelly, "The CEO's Second Wife: Yes, She's Typically Younger Than the First. Often She Has a Career of Her Own. But Her Primary Job Is Remaking His Life. Sometimes the Change He Undergoes Even Results in His Becoming a More Considerate Manager," *Fortune*, August 28, 1989, p. 52.

increasingly CEOs are ditching their first wives for younger, newer "models," much like trading in an old car for a new one. True, the "newer ones" are better educated, more likely to run their own businesses, etc. It is also the case, however, that they are both younger and prettier, which constitutes their main qualifications. However, the real point is that a number of the CEOs who were interviewed for the article felt that they were "entitled to their new wives." They had "earned it" by having worked so hard and attaining a top spot in society.

Consequences for Crisis Management:

In most organizations, the Resourcism game influences the basic use of language—more fundamentally still how we "think about reality"—in that we speak of "financial resources," "natural resources," or even "human resources." The Resourcism game can be seen as another expression of the Fragmentation game where nature, people, and objects are viewed only from the perspective of their ability to be used or consumed as an object. In the area of CM, the Resourcism game has a strong impact on the overall decrease of ethics and human dignity issues in business decisions. Nature and people are seen only as "resources," and to be treated as such.

Resourcism games are often connected to a deeper sense of ethnocentricity where some individuals see others as inferior to themselves and rationalize their exploitation as an inherent "right" or "entitlement." The history of industrial activities is filled with countless examples of ethnocentricity. For example, during the Industrial Revolution authors as diverse as Dickens and Marx denounced the exploitation of children and women in factory work and the general exploitation of workers. Today the Resourcism game is directed toward two groups in particular, Third World countries and women.

The exploitation of the Third World by industrial nations is a subject that is almost never discussed in Crisis-Prone organizations. However, it is clear that at the present time the gap between rich and poor countries is widening not narrowing. Even more strongly, a recent international study commissioned by the United Nations[6] emphasized that the current economic growth of industrial countries has been

6. *The World Commission on Environment and Development, Our Common Future.* The United Nations, New York: Oxford University Press, 1987.

achieved, particularly in the last ten years, largely at the expense of poorer countries through their systematic exploitation instead of through the development of innovations in the industrialized nations themselves. The study also warns of the potential crises that the situation could create in the area of national security. In the near future, Third World nations could revolt against their inhuman conditions and retaliate against developed and rich countries through acts of terrorism.

The ethnocentricity of Crisis-Prone organizations is also directed toward the employment of women. It is now well documented that women earn about one-third less than men for equal work.[7] In addition, they experience greater difficulty in gaining access to more interesting and prestigious jobs. Women are also exploited in another way in Crisis-Prone organizations: through sexual abuse and harassment. Recent studies indicate that two out of three male executives in *Fortune* 500 organizations[8] have extramarital affairs either at work or during business trips. Putting aside the moral and ethical implications of these acts, it is important to note that the greater the engagement in Sexual games in Crisis-Prone organizations, the greater the increase in other crises. In a recent survey we conducted it was found that issues of sexual harassment were considered by the responding companies as their seventh largest crisis out of a total of twenty-one. We have encountered more than one male executive who kept an organizational chart of his "female conquests." While more data is certainly necessary on so critical an issue, it seems that one of the most powerful ways to evaluate the crisis potential of any organization is to evaluate the degree to which it engages in Resourcism games and their impact on the environment in general and women in particular.

Game Breakers:

Crisis-Prepared organizations play the Resourcism game far less. This does not mean that they respect all environmental regulations or that they are entirely free of sexual harassment. Rather, the point is that, as with all the other games, they have developed explicit programs to evaluate and police their behavior.

---

7. Jan Halper, *Quiet Desperation, the Truth About Successful Men*. New York: Warner, 1988.
8. *Ibid.*

16. The "Bigger Is Better" Game

Deep Motivation:

The Bigger Is Better game is played from deep wishes for protection, invulnerability, omnipotence, and inner strength. This game is played out of deep feelings of fragmentation as well as inner fragility. Sadly enough, the games are reinforced by traditional economic theory with its emphasis on constant growth and "economies of scale."

General Signs and Consequences for Crisis Management:

Perhaps the most visible sign of the importance of this game is in the extreme positive value given to the concept of growth in American society as a whole. In contrast to Japanese firms, U.S. organizations are under constant pressure to produce bigger and better profits. However, the deeper cause of this game can be seen in the narcissism that is so endemic in American society. If one has an organization of 50 people which generates a profit of $50 million a year, then an organization of 200 with a profit of $500 million is even better. No matter what the avenue or area of expression in American society, it is generally felt that on every dimension "bigger is better." What is often left out of this equation is the fact that in today's world, the sheer magnification of the scale of a product, service, or process can often lead to disastrous, unintended effects or consequences.

On every front of our lives, it is becoming clearer and clearer that instead of "bigger or more leading to more," the exact reverse is the case.[9] Increasingly, "bigger or more leads to less." We have reached a point of saturation where bigness has become its own worst enemy.

Game Breakers:

Executives in Crisis-Prepared organizations realize that many of the technologies that they depend on have become far too complex and large for them to manage safely. Three different strategies have been developed in order to deal with this: (1) to decrease wherever possible the size and complexity of their technical systems; (2) to increase the

---

9. See Ian I. Mitroff, *Business Not as Usual. Rethinking Our Individual, Corporate, and Industrial Strategies for Global Competition*. San Francisco Jossey-Bass: 1988.

corresponding ability of their managers and executives to handle and manage complexity; and (3) to design explicitly—not leave to chance—the appropriate management control systems capable of recognizing and managing these complexities.

17. The "Faster Is Better" Game

Deep Motivation:

The motivation for this and the previous game are the following: take any attribute or property of existence and increase or magnify that property as much as possible; supposedly desirable ends will follow almost automatically. As such, this and the preceding game are associated strongly with deep feelings of the desire for omnipotence, and at an even deeper level, of corresponding feelings of inadequacy. These games are also associated with the need to ward off intense feelings of boredom. This game is especially reinforced by all the competitive pressures that now exist in a global economy, especially with the increased fears for any organization's ability to survive.

General Signs:

One of the clearest signs of the importance of this game can be seen in a 1988 *Fortune* magazine cover story which stated that innovative companies have discovered the virtues of "speed." Some companies reducing their R&D budgets and production times by some 400 percent.[10] The importance of this game is also demonstrated by the marked general increase in executive stress.

Consequences for Crisis Management:

Both this game and the previous one contradict Charles Perrow's[11] notion of the tight coupling that now exists in complex technical systems: the more that a system is tightly coupled to others, the more likely it is to collapse, not to survive. Thus, the increasing potential for industrial disasters. Perhaps no better example exists than the 1987 crash of the stock market. Computerized information systems precipitously speeded up the decisions to buy and to sell stocks at larger

10. "How Managers Can Succeed Through Speed," *Fortune*, February 13, 1989, pp. 54-66.
11. Charles Perrow, *Normal Accidents*. New York: Basic Books, 1984.

volumes than had ever been experienced before.

Game Breakers:

Executives in Crisis-Prepared organizations recognize that *slow and small can be just as beautiful as big and fast.* For example, as we have stressed repeatedly, in our many interviews related to the Hinsdale IBT communication disaster we found a number of companies that have attempted to decrease their dependency on information technology.

IMAGE GAMES

18. The "Magician's" or "Illusion" Game

Deep Motivation:

This game is perhaps the single best expression of the desire for omnipotence across almost all of the games we have discussed. It springs from the deep belief that "sleight of hands" and quick fixes will make all problems disappear. This game is especially reinforced, not only by the general rise of professionalism in our society as well as the Faster Is Better game, but by the general narcissism and the extreme focus on image over reality. In addition, the Magician's game provides its players with the illusion of playing with the "big boys," dealing with millions of dollars as opposed again to focusing on real substantive business issues.

General Signs:

Robert Reich, for one, has denounced the dangers of "paper entrepreneurialism."[12] The manipulation of stocks and the proliferation of takeovers have not added generally to the substantive wealth or productive capacity of American society. Further, the number of attorneys in the U.S. has increased by some 68 percent in the last decade while the number of engineers has only increased by some 15 percent.[13] In other words, more energy in our society is currently put into

12. Robert Reich, *The Next American Frontier*. New York: Times Books, 1983.
13. *Ibid.*, p. 159.

Get Even, Image, and Accumulation games rather than into activities that contribute to productivity. Further, in 1985 the combined expenditures for R&D and net nonresidential investments were below the record levels of mergers and acquisitions which reached a sum of $190 billion in 1986!

This game in particular engages executives in Crisis-Prone organizations in making shallow changes as opposed to real change. The investment in changes which are shallow is associated directly with the internal shallowness characteristic of far too many executives.

Consequences for Crisis Management:

The basic purpose of such games is to add to a feeling of security and safety. They are a demonstration of Hecate's work at its worst. Examples can be found everywhere. For instance, in 1987 General Motors chose not to address an obvious transmission problem, preferring instead to settle the case for $19.2 million and repurchasing a few days later $5 billion of its own common stock, thereby artificially increasing its price.

Game Breakers:

Executives in Crisis-Prepared organizations recognize that there are no magical solutions or quick fixes to real problems. They do not delude themselves or dilute their energies by playing games that do not result in dealing with substantive issues but choose instead to place their energies into the development of a number of products and services that can compete in the marketplace.

19. The "I Should Always Look Good" Game

Deep Motivation:

This game is played out of the desire to experience an illusionary sense of perfection and omnipotence. It also springs from a deeply felt sense of inner inadequacy, and is reinforced by the different and constant demands from organizations for managers to be reliable, professional, competent, self-assured, etc.

General Signs:

A sign of the importance of such games is the proliferation of "perfect" resumes by executives in Crisis-Prone organizations. Certain executives, it seems, are always making the "right career moves at the right time at the right place." They have mastered the art of the "continual presentation of oneself in a positive light by downplaying their failures.

Consequences for Crisis Management:

Such games require executives in Crisis-Prone organizations to involve themselves only with tasks that have a great chance of success, heightened visibility, and short-term payoffs. As a result, they do not involve themselves with operations which, while they may be far more reliable, often require a long-term commitment. They also avoid those projects which lack dramatic visibility and whose success is uncertain. They do not involve themselves with tasks that could challenge or go against the desire of top management. In every sense, they reinforce the status quo. Lastly, long after such executives have left, others are often surprised by the number of lingering "time bombs" that have been left around. One of the most puzzling phenomena associated with this game is the tendency of those who play it to insist upon always appearing to be "flexible." Exhorted to be flexible at all costs by management gurus in order to survive, the I Should Always Look Good game leads individuals, paradoxically, to be "rigidly committed to change."

Game Breakers:

While concerned about their careers, executives in Crisis-Prepared organizations are also deeply committed to the organization as a whole and to jobs well done. They have developed the emotional capacity for whistle-blowing, sometimes risking their very position, as in the example of Roger Biojoly with regard to the Challenger disaster. Crisis-Prepared organizations attempt to make the "invisibility" of reliable or taken-for-granted products, technology, systems, etc., visible again through various mechanisms such as bonus plans, awards, promotions, etc.

20. The "Image" Game

Deep Motivation:

This game is deeply associated with the Magician's game. This game, however, focuses in particular on the importance of communication for convincing others that one is "perfect" and should be readily admired by others. As we shall see later when we talk about societal games, this one is reinforced especially by the incredible importance that is placed on image as part of our general "TV society."

General Signs:

The fundamental purpose of the Image game is to make everyone believe that superficial images and looks are more important than real actions based on substantive worth and accomplishments. To a certain extent, this game has especially been played by politicians in the latter part of this century. Former President Nixon's behavior provides a clear example. The actual content and substance of his speeches were far less important than the results they obtained as measured by polls. Thus, a "bad" speech was not measured by its "faulty content," but rather by whether it contributed to a "increased credibility gap." Even after Watergate, Nixon truly believed that his "credibility gap" could have been corrected by a good speech. Having been a professional actor, Ronald Reagan may turn out to have been the greatest master of this particular game. Many have contended with great justification that Reagan's best performance as an actor was his presidency.

Consequences for Crisis Management:

The importance of the Image game in CM can be measured by the recent importance that has been given to public relations. A survey we did of 281 articles published on CM from 1960 to mid-1988 found that more than 40 percent dealt specifically with different public relations strategies while less than 15 percent dealt with substantive strategies. This is not to say that public relations should be ignored as an important area in CM. PR, public affairs, and communications are important aspects of all crises. The point is that at the present time executives in Crisis-Prone organizations are much more interested in finding the "right" communications approach for defending themselves *after* a disaster than in focusing on substantive steps that they can engage in to lessen the chances of a crisis occurring *before* it happens.

Game Breakers:

Executives in Crisis-Prepared organizations understand the necessity of good public relations and public affairs. However, they focus much more on what they can do before a crisis occurs to lower its chances of occurring.

CONCLUDING REMARKS

The greatest irony connected with the games we have described in this and the last chapter is that those who possess even the most minimal awareness of them are the ones who suffer most. These are indeed the "tragic" souls that we discussed in Chapter 2. They not only realize but profoundly feel the absurdity of their lives. "Destructive" souls on the other hand are not even vaguely aware of their behavior. They live in what may be called an "innocence of evil."

Contrary to those whose behavior and lives are tragic or destructive, healthy souls have both the capacity to see the dangers of busyness games as well as the moral and emotional strength to stop playing them. This does not mean that those whose behavior we label "healthy" are thereby perfect and that they never engage in the games we have identified. To the contrary! All of us engage in such games since we all suffer from the same dilemmas of the human condition. The difference is that healthy individuals are far more able to face anxiety straight on, and as a result, to derive substantial fulfillment from their work to the benefit of their families, communities, and society as a whole. Healthy individuals are also much more able to realize that one can not and should not escape all feelings of anxiety altogether. Although often painful, all feelings, especially disturbing ones, constitute the basis of human freedom and creativity. Without them, we would not be motivated to improve the human condition.

For these reasons, we need to explore the phenomenon of anxiety a bit more. Feelings of anxiety lie at the very core of what we have referred to as "character defects." In a nutshell, anxiety is experienced as a feeling of inner conflict or subjective turmoil. As such, it corresponds to the feelings of inner and subjective fragmentation that we described in Chapter 2. Feelings of anxiety are so basic that, virtually without exception, all of the founders of modern psychology have argued that they constitute *the* starting point for modern, scientific studies of the "soul." For example, Freud argued that anxiety is the fundamental phenomenon and the central problem of neurosis.[14]

Three things in particular need to be made clear about the phenomenon of anxiety. *First*, we are not concerned here with *fear* since fear and anxiety are in general two very different things. To a certain extent, fear is objectified. One is afraid *of something*. To use a simple example, if upon waking one morning and going downstairs you saw an actual tiger in your kitchen, then you would indeed be justified in experiencing fear. You would in fact be out of touch with reality and your feelings if you did not experience fear. In contrast, anxiety is not objectified. One is not anxious *of something*. Anxiety is a subjective "state of being," an "inner turmoil."

To be anxious is "to feel threatened from all sides at once" precisely because one does not know the exact direction from which an attack will come, if at all. This is not to say that anxiety is never associated with real or specific threats. Rather, anxiety is experienced because of things that either caused or were associated with fear in the past. Thus, threats due to industrial disasters like Bhopal or Exxon Valdez are not responsible for causing anxiety per se. Instead, they activate whatever past associations still linger in our minds with regard to whatever fears we may once have experienced and which need only the barest energy in order to be reactivated. To borrow a metaphor from Rollo May, the organized attacks of an enemy from specific geographical locations can legitimately be associated with fear.[15] In contrast, if an enemy has already penetrated the walls of one's city or fortress and is engaged in conducting guerrilla activities everywhere, then this is more than sufficient to produce anxiety. The threat originating from "everywhere" challenges the very core or existence of the city itself. Hecate herself was believed to have practiced her magic at the intersection of roads, symbolizing that her work could be seen in every direction, to all sides at once, thus meeting the central core of the definition of anxiety.

Second, stress and anxiety are also two different things. The con-

---

14. See for instance, Sigmund Freud, *Group Psychology and Analysis of the Ego*. London: Hogart, 1921; and Sigmund Freud, *Totem and Taboo, Some Points of Agreement Between the Mental Lives of Savages and Neurotics*. New York: Norton, 1950.
15. Rollo May, *The Meaning of Anxiety*. New York: Washington Square Press, 1950.

cept of "stress" has been borrowed largely from the field of engineering. It has received extensive recognition in recent years since stress can be defined and measured much more precisely than diffuse experiences of anxiety. Stress is related more to forces external to people. Anxiety on the other hand refers more to one's total experience of *inner* turmoil. To some extent, we can say that *anxiety reflects how we handle stress*, i.e., how we perceive and relate to stressful events such as industrial crises. Also, stress and anxiety are not always reciprocal. It is possible to be highly stressed and yet not be anxious, as is often the case with professional athletes during the excitement of a sporting event. For another, studies in wartime indicate that when people are under severe stress due to bombing, acute austerity, etc., there is a clear *decline* in neuroses. This somewhat puzzling phenomenon can be explained by the fact that stressful situations allow individuals to pinpoint their inner turmoil and objectify their feelings of anxiety—as in fear.

Third, we also need to distinguish between "healthy" and "neurotic" anxiety. Healthy anxiety is characterized by four different criteria.

- One, the anxiety is appropriate to the threat, as in the case of the tiger. Healthy people are not immune to anxiety. Healthy executives are appropriately concerned with such major threatening issues as increased competition, the survival of their organizations, environmental issues, or major industrial disasters. Outside of work, healthy anxiety is related to such issues as nuclear war, the rise of crime, drug abuse, etc.
- Two, healthy anxiety does not require repression. Healthy individuals have the strength of character to allow themselves to be anxious about appropriate threats.
- Three, healthy anxiety is used productively. Recognizing the appropriate nature of the threat, healthy individuals can use their feelings of anxiety as a springboard for creativity and innovation. In the particular area of crises, healthy executives are able to create a number of innovative strategies for reducing both the likelihood of crises and their impact.
- Four, healthy anxiety does not lead to major physical symptoms such as heart attacks or ulcers.

In contrast, neurotic anxiety is not appropriate to the threat and does require repression. For example, during the conduct of our interviews we met executives who denied vehemently the existence of real problems. One, for instance, denied the 70 percent yearly turnover of employees was a real problem for his organization. In essence, the problem was defined out of existence by saying that "a 70 percent yearly turnover of employees is normal." For another, we have also encountered executives for whom "murder was just one of the costs of doing business in crime ridden neighborhoods." For still another, a major telecommunications breakdown involving a half-million customers for several days was also viewed as "normal."

Signs of the increase in anxiety and threats to the "self" of executives in organizations are now numerous. As such, they echo the present situation that is widely felt throughout society as a whole. Companies express more and more concern with how they are perceived by their external stakeholders. In a recent analysis of the corporate statements of sixty-one of the *Fortune* 500 companies,[16] the top four concerns mentioned were: (1) survival (90 percent of the respondents); (2) desirable public image (86 percent); (3) clear expression of basic beliefs and philosophy (79 percent); and, (4) desirable self-concept of the company (77 percent). If these do indeed reflect concerns which are essentially existential in nature, then more traditional, substantive issues of business such as what to produce and where and how to sell it were mentioned far less: commitment to principal products and services (67 percent); reaching intended targeted customers and markets (48 percent); reaching intended geographic areas of business (41 percent); definition of core technology (20 percent). This trend is also evident in the present increase in public relations efforts to define an appropriate "corporate identity" for many organizations. While it is of course normal that every organization be concerned with its external image, we believe nonetheless that many public relations efforts are directed more toward creating an artificial image in order to cover up internal deficiencies.

Drug abuse has also increased dramatically in all organizations. In a recent *Fortune* cover story,[17] a medical director who was in charge of 160 hospitals declared that "drugs have taken the business world by storm." Another example can be found in a recent *Business Week* cover

16. J. A. Pearce and F. David, "Corporate Mission Statements: the Bottom Line," *Academy of Management Executive*, Vol. 1, November 2, 1987, pp. 109-116.
17. ———, "The Executive Addict," *Fortune*, June 24, 1985, pp. 24-31.

story[18] entitled "Fast-Track Kids," which described the characteristics of "hot" MBAs entering major U.S. corporations. While the author described them as "better educated, more self-confident, and less fearful," she also stressed their darker side as well: their inability to delay gratification, their lack of empathy for others, their lack of commitment and loyalty to the firm or anyone else.

The admiration and idealization of grandiose and flamboyant leaders is also significantly on the rise both within and outside of organizations. A number of social critics have denounced such behavior and the idealization of it by the public. Robert Reich has denounced the myth of the "triumphant individual"[19] who can "either be Rambo, Ronald Reagan, or Gary Cooper in another era." Similarly, Warren Bennis has argued that idolatry has gone to the heads of CEOs at the expense of the entire American public.[20] The recent biographies of "leaders" such as Iacocca, Trump, and Goldsmith have remained on *The New York Times* best-seller list for months. It would seem that at the present time a large part of the American public has fallen in love with such leaders, choosing not to focus as they once did on their moral qualities or their substantive characteristics or the products and services they once championed. Rather, the public now idealizes the image and the imagery of omnipotence, power, and grandiosity, and the gluttonous wealth that such leaders project. What seems to matter more at the present time is not to produce a product or a service that one can be proud of, but instead to become rich, powerful, and famous in the illusion that wealth, power, and fame will eliminate whatever feelings of anxiety persist at one's core.

Of course, not all managers and professionals use the mechanisms we have described. Unfortunately, this does not lead us to conclude that the situation may be better than that which we have observed. Other studies have uncovered concerns that are very similar to those that we have observed. Some of them have noted the very same sense of despair among executives. In her book *Quiet Desperation* Jan Halper, after personally interviewing more than 4,000 *Fortune* 500 executives over a period of six years, emphasized their overall sense of despair as well as their need to implement change quietly and in isolation.

18. ——, "Fast Track Kids," *Business Week*, November 10, 1986.
19. Robert B. Reich, *Tales of a New America*. New York: Times Books, 1987.
20. Warren Bennis, *On Becoming a Leader*. Redding, MA: Addison-Wesley, 1989.

When executives in Crisis-Prone organizations emphasize the
need for their companies to develop more effective CM plans and procedures, they overwhelmingly stressed their deep sense of isolation,
despair, and lack of support from their very own organizations. An
executive in a large food organization declared that he was the "only
executive in his company who worried about such issues." Another
executive in a large telecommunications firm stressed that he had to
develop "underground programs" because he was limited by his relative lack of power and access to resources. This executive also emphasized that this was one of the only ways for him to develop appropriate
CM efforts without threatening his job. Another executive in a major
airline stated that in a number of areas his company was literally
"walking on the edge of a major catastrophe," but he could neither
discuss such issues with his executive group nor did he have the resources to remedy the situation.

Because of what we have observed, we believe that most programs of stress management and other such quick-fix gimmicks are
mostly a sham! Not only do they not fix the problems for which they
are intended, but they actually make things even worse by reinforcing
the status quo through the illusion that people are actually working on
the real issues at hand. This is why we have focused so strongly on the
games we have described. If the top members of an organization play
games, then as the prime bearers and embodiments of their culture,
they literally set the moral tone for the entire organization. The games
they play constitute a far more powerful message than all the fancy
memos and proclamations they make. The games send a clear signal as
to what the real values of the organization are. If this is the case, then
it should come as no surprise to see why it is so difficult to change any
organization, let alone ones that are truly troubled. To change an organization means coming to grips with the fact that games exist as well as
with the incredible power and hold that they have over everyone connected with the organization.

Because of what we have seen and described, it would seem therefore that there is virtually no hope whatsoever. If it seems that breaking out of such games is difficult—and it is—then it also needs to be
said that it is not impossible. Some of the greatest feelings of pride,
energy, and creativity are released when an organization directly con-
fronts its games and breaks out of them.

Part II

ORGANIZATIONAL GAMES

Chapter 5

Mega-Arrogance: Games That Organizations Play

Everything bad that happens happens because of a conscious, intelligent concerted ill-will.

Artaud

. . . Drinking has been an important part of Hazelwood's life since his college days, but it did not impede a rapid rise to the top of Exxon's seafaring ranks. *Hazelwood long seemed to believe that nothing bad could befall him* [emphasis ours]. As the ironic motto printed next to his picture in his college yearbook put it, "It can't happen to me."

Scott Brown,
"Joe's Bad Trip," *Time*,
July 24, 1989, p. 47

Johnny Carson and Ed McMahon are tops at what they do. They have refined their comedy to an art. Their most successful routines are so well known that a few choice words or gestures are enough to invoke anticipation of the whole routine. They especially seem to enjoy themselves in one routine where Ed typically picks up a piece of paper, waves it dramatically, and then exclaims in a highly stylized voice reminiscent of W. C. Fields, "On this very piece of paper is every conceivable thing you would ever want to know about Jim and Tammy Bakker's deep devotion to one another." Without missing a beat, Johnny gives Ed one of his wry, sardonic smiles and says something like, "Not so, buffalo breath!" The scene dissolves into laughter. The bit continues with Johnny giving additional off-the-wall items that were not on Ed's original list.

The subject matter of this book is anything but a laughing matter. If it is a joke, then it is not only on those organizations that cause crises, but increasingly on all of us as the recipients of their actions and inactions. If there is any similarity between Johnny and Ed's comic routines and our subject matter, it lies in the fact that over the years we have heard just about every rationalization there is as to why organizations need not take crisis prevention seriously. Their consequences are so serious that we need to examine them.

In recent years, those who study and help organizations change have come to appreciate and to systematically explore a deeper set of forces that guide the behavior of all organizations. No one disputes that factors such as the context in which a firm competes, the structure of its industry—whether it is regulated or deregulated—its financial status, its capital and plant requirements all influence an organization's behavior. In addition to these more overt and conscious factors, it has also been found that a set of much less observable, largely unconscious factors exert a strong, if not a decisive, effect on the behavior of all organizations. These additional factors are referred to as the "culture" of an organization.[1]

The culture of an organization may be generally defined as the set of rarely articulated, largely unconscious, taken-for-granted beliefs, values, norms, and fundamental assumptions the organization makes about itself, the nature of people in general, and its environment. In effect, culture constitutes the set of "unwritten rules" that govern "acceptable behavior" within and even outside of the organization. For instance, an organization's culture may prescribe such unwritten rules as: "If you want to succeed around here, don't disagree with the boss" or "Don't be the bearer of bad news" or "Don't share information with rival groups within the organization; your first loyalty is to your own immediate work group, not to others." On the positive side, innovative organizations often have such norms as: "The best ideas are those that 'rock the boat'"; "You won't be fired for making 'creative'

---

1. For an introduction to the literature on organizational culture, which is by now vast, see Ralph H. Kilmann, *Beyond the Quick-Fix. Managing Five Tracks to Organizational Success*. San Francisco, CA: Jossey-Bass, 1984; E. H. Schein, *Organizational Culture and Leadership*. San Francisco, CA: Jossey-Bass, 1985.

mistakes as long as you keep open lines of communication with superiors."

Corporate culture affects what is considered as "acceptable" — styles of dress; proper modes of talk; body language; how one socializes and with whom; who is and is not considered a hero, villain, victim; who's in, who's out; where to live; whom to marry; where to go to school; who to eat lunch with, and so on.

The rationalizations that we have heard in the course of our interviews are indicative of the general feeling, tone or mindset of an organization. They reveal how seriously an organization really takes crisis preparedness. Far too many organizations kid themselves that they are Crisis Prepared by having tons of equipment sitting in yards, volumes of manuals sitting on shelves, rule after rule, tons of regulations, procedures, and so forth. To an outsider, the organization thus seems well prepared. However, those on the inside are not fooled; they know that the surface is all sham. It is all a game to fool everyone and ultimately no one.

Before we begin, we need to address an important consideration. Because the vast majority of the information we obtained was collected under strict promises of confidentiality, in no case can we mention either the names of the individuals or the organizations that were involved in our interviews. The only organizations we mention by name are those like Johnson & Johnson, Morton-Thiokol, Union Carbide, NASA, and Exxon which have already been examined publicly in the media. Because much of the information we collected is extremely damaging both to the individuals and to the organizations involved, we cannot in good conscience "name names."

It should be understood that what follows is based on our over 350 interviews with top executives in over 120 organizations. The individuals and the organizations studied span nearly every type of industry. We have every reason to believe that they are representative of the general thinking of corporate America with regard to crisis management (CM). In addition, our results seem representative not only of corporate America but also of the situation encountered in most developed nations, since in the thirty or so interviews that have been conducted so far in Canada, the same patterns have been found. Also, our interview results have been supplemented by questionnaires that have surveyed the feelings and attitudes of a much wider body of corporate opinion. In most cases, the executives interviewed were the top individuals in their organizations directly concerned with overseeing crisis management. In many cases, they disagreed strongly with the views of their superiors when they were asked to respond to such questions as: Is CM really taken seriously around here? What are the general beliefs in your organization that either support or inhibit effective crisis management? How would you describe the general culture of your organization? How does it either support or inhibit effective crisis management?

The rationalizations we've heard fall "broadly" into four main groups: (1) special properties or characteristics of an organization that supposedly make it immune to crises; (2) special properties of the environment that make it immune; (3) special properties of crises themselves; and (4) special properties with regard to how the organization has handled past crises that supposedly make it immune from future crises (see table 1). The word "broadly" is appropriate here since as we encountered in our previous discussion of games, there is a great deal of overlap between the four groups.

No organization appears to subscribe to, at least not the ones we've encountered, all thirty-one rationalizations at once. However, the greater the number of rationalizations that are subscribed to, the more Crisis-Prone an organization is. Finally, since many of the rationalizations are self-explanatory, we shall not comment directly on every one of them.

1. The Fallacy of Size

Looks are almost always deceiving. It would be nice if there were a quick and simple way by which one could spot a Crisis-Prone organization just by walking in the front door and gauging its appearance by means of the lavishness of its decor, the opulence of its architecture, and so forth. True, there are some tip-offs, but so many organizations nowadays—public as well as private—project an image of grandiosity, power, and wealth that it is impossible by sheer observation alone to spot a Crisis-Prone organization.

For our purposes, the real proof, however strange this may sound, lies "in the words," especially if they are widely voiced and shared by members throughout an organization. We've listed the rationalization "Our size will protect us from a major disaster or crisis" as first on our list since in nearly every organization we have diagnosed as Crisis Prone, in one form or another, this belief is present. *However ex-*

Table 1

Faulty Rationalizations That Can Seriously Harm
an Organization and Its Environment

Group 1 Properties of the Organization That Will Protect It From Crises	Group 2 Properties of the Environment That Will Protect It	Group 3 Properties of Crises Themselves	Group 4 Properties of How We Have Handled Crises in the Past That Will Protect Us From Future Crises
1) Our Size Will Protect Us	11) If a Major Crisis Happens, Someone Else Will Rescue Us	17) Most Crises Turn Out Not to Be Very Important	24) Crisis Management Is Like an Insurance Policy; You Only Need to Buy So Much
2) Excellent, Well-Managed Companies Do Not Have Crises	12) Crisis Management Is Someone Else's Responsibility	18) Each Crisis Is So Unique That It Is Not Possible to Prepare for Them	25) In a Crisis Situation, We Just Need to Refer to the Emergency Procedures We've Laid Out in Our Crisis Manuals
3) Our Special Location Will Protect Us	13) The Environment Is Benign, or, We Can Effectively Buffer Ourselves From the Environment	19) Crises Are Solely Negative in Their Impacts	26) We Are a Team That Will Function Well During a Crisis
4) Certain Crises Only Happen to Others		20) Crises Are Isolated	27) Only Executives Need to Be Aware of Our Crisis Plans; Why Scare Our Employees or Members of the Community?
5) Crises Do Not Require Special Procedures	14) Nothing New Has Really Occurred That Warrants Change	21) Most, If Not All, Crises Have a Technical Solution	
6) It Is Enough to React to a Crisis Once It Has Happened	15) It's Not a Crisis If It Doesn't Happen to or Hurt Us	22) It's Enough to Throw Technical and Financial Quick Fixes at a Problem	28) The Only Important Thing in Crisis Management Is to Make Sure That Our Internal Operations Stay Intact
7) Crisis Management or Crisis Prevention Is a Luxury	16) Crime/Murder Is Just a Cost of Doing Business	23) Most Crises Resolve Themselves; Therefore Time Is Our Best Ally	
8) Employees Who Bring Bad News Deserve to Be Punished			29) We Are Tough Enough to React to a Crisis in an Objective and Rational Manner
9) Desirable Business Ends Justify the Taking of High-Risk Means			30) We Know How to Manipulate the Media
10) Our Employees Are So Dedicated That We Can Trust Them Without Question			31) The Most Important Thing in Crisis Management Is to Protect the Good Image of the Organization Through Public Relations and Advertising Campaigns

pressed, the belief that an organization is immune or exempt from a major crisis is the cornerstone of a Crisis-Prone organization. Anyone who either works for, has significant contact with, or has an investment in such an organization ought to get as far away from it as quickly as possible. Sooner or later such an organization is destined to cause or be involved in a major crisis.

At its root, the belief that the size of one's organization will protect it from a major crisis is a crude, but nonetheless, blunt expression of the arrogance of power. Alternate expressions reveal this sentiment even more strongly:

"Our sheer size will shield us from a major crisis";
"We're so big and powerful that in reality nothing could actually bring us down."

It is amazing to witness this belief in action and how truly persistent it is. Senior executives who have sat through detailed discussions of CM, nodding their heads repeatedly in agreement at every one of the points that were made about the extreme danger in believing in any of the rationalizations that are discussed in this chapter, have approached us at some point in the proceedings and remarked, "But you know in actuality there is very little that could bring down an organization of our size, power, etc." What the proponents of this view fail to comprehend is that while what they say might be true of them—there may well be no crisis big or critical enough to bring *them* down—their organization's beliefs could nonetheless help to cause a crisis that will bring down *those around them.* No better example could be given than Exxon Valdez. Exxon is indeed so big, so powerful, so arrogant that little, if anything, may be able to bring them down. But as we have witnessed, this attitude is enough to cause extreme damage to the environment.

Notice that what we are saying challenges strongly the perspective of orthodox economists who maintain that the only responsibility of a corporation is to its major shareholders. Industrial crises constitute terrifying proof in themselves that an organization has a responsibility to all its *stakeholders,* which include its employees, its customers, as well as, more generally, all the members of its surrounding community. Furthermore, industrial crises also demonstrate very painfully that organizations also have a tremendous responsibility toward innocent bystanders—those who may never have even heard of the organization before and whose only relation to it is by means of their close physical proximity to it. They have a responsibility to the millions of people in Europe who were affected by the Chernobyl disaster, or the countless animals and vegetation in Valdez, Alaska.

One of the first important findings we uncovered in the area of CM was that Crisis-Prone versus Crisis-Prepared organizations had very different definitions of what constituted a crisis. The differences were so striking that they were the first tip-off to the critical differences in the belief systems of the two respective kinds of organizations. A crisis for a Crisis-Prone organization is something that affects *them*, e.g., *their* products, *their* top executives. On the other hand, a crisis for a Crisis-Prepared organization is something that affects not only them personally but also their customers, their surrounding communities, the families of their employees, and their general environment. The greatest distinction between these two types of organizations is in precisely this: how they relate to those outside of them, and particularly to those who do not have the same kind of power they have, e.g., the unborn and future generations. For Crisis-Prone organizations, the powerless tend either not to exist or their importance is discounted entirely.

This observation helps to explain the following: Crisis-Prone organizations generally confuse their own internal operating structure with the structure of the environment in which they operate. More often than not, executives in Crisis-Prone organizations engage in long and bloody political battles over the competition for resources, power, or status. As a result, their conception of the world is literally that of a "battlefield," where every inch of the land is gained and held through sheer force and power. Individuals who are conditioned by such an environment naturally develop a "jungle outlook," a jungle where survival is the only reason and motivation for existence. For such people, those who have little or no power or capability for conducting battle do not exist.

Furthermore, those who have been constantly conditioned by the endless search for and maintenance of power feel that those who are lacking in power should not even be considered "human." Thus, powerless individuals are to be used as an impersonal resource, much in the manner that one uses a piece of land or a gallon of oil. Powerless individuals are to be deprived of all their basic human rights, not to mention dignity. If only for this reason, destructive Crisis-Prone organizations not only deserve the same contempt in which they regard others, but deserve to be strongly regulated and their top executives punished by law.

The behaviors described in the preceding paragraph are a restatement of many of the behaviors we have encountered earlier in describing the games that individuals play. Thus, it is all the more important to emphasize that in this chapter we are primarily describing the behavior of entire organizations, not necessarily that of single individuals. Although, to be sure, there are strong overlaps between them, the two are not necessarily the same. The thing that is so spooky about groups, organizations, and even whole cultures is that large groups of people often act in ways that isolated individuals on their own would not. Thus, even though many of the descriptions in this chapter sound the same—and indeed are the same—it must be borne constantly in mind that we are describing beliefs and actions that apply primarily to the mindset of an entire organization. Thus, for instance, the very rationalizations that we have uncovered were not necessarily held by many of the individuals we interviewed. Instead, they were imputed as "general beliefs of the organization as a whole."

We've listed this particular rationalization first because it is not only one of the single most important forces responsible for causing a major crisis in the first place, but also one of the most important forces responsible for keeping an organization from changing so that it will not produce new crises in the future. How can an organization, like an individual, possibly change if it does not accept responsibility for its actions, or even partial responsibility for them?

11. The Fallacy of Protection or Resource Abundance

Rationalization in group two is the mirror image or counterpart to rationalization eleven in group one. (This is the reason why we discuss it next instead of number two.) If number one is characteristic of those organizations that assume the role of Big Bully, then number eleven is characteristic of those that exist in a childlike state of dependency with regard to someone bigger than themselves. They are protected, so they hope, by the Big Bullies of the world from other bullies. Hence their persistent belief: "If something bad happens, someone else bigger and better than us will come to our rescue, absorb our losses, bail us out, etc." Beliefs such as these are especially characteristic of those organizations that have grown up and lived most of their existence in a regulated or quasi-regulated environment. Utilities and organizations such as banks, airlines, hospitals, etc., are typically the ones that have not only subscribed to this belief historically but have even prospered as a consequence of holding it. Today's rapidly changing environment is forcing, often with much pain, those organizations that have survived up to this point to question the continued validity of such beliefs.

It is important to emphasize once again the psychological hold that rationalizations one and eleven have on the people who work for the organizations that espouse such beliefs. Those who work for organizations which are characterized by their allegiance to rationalization number one experience a need, much of it unconscious, to be associated with power. This need goes far beyond "mere association." As we have seen in previous chapters, the bigness of the organization substitutes for the general feeling of powerlessness, and even of emptiness, on the inside of many of those, especially at the top, who work within such organizations. The organization becomes a substitute for the weak, deficient, and undeveloped parts of the person's personality.

It is also just as important to understand that although the rationalizations espoused and the purposes they serve are virtually the same as those we have encountered in our previous discussion of the games that individuals play, in the present case we are describing the game behaviors that entire organizations play, not necessarily that of individuals. To a certain extent it is possible—at least theoretically—to be a member of a destructive or tragic organization without thereby being or becoming a destructive or tragic individual. What is not possible is to remain unaffected. The more that one disagrees with or is in opposition to the organization, the greater the stress one experiences and suffers. Indeed, there is an interesting body of evidence which suggests that it is precisely the "healthier" individuals who suffer the most in destructive organizations and not the more overtly "dysfunctional or sick" members.[2]

Those who work for organizations that espouse rationalization number eleven on the other hand don't even seek empowerment in the first place. They are primarily seeking refuge and protection from a complex, harsh world. There is in fact an unspoken anxiety that drives such organizations and their members. There is the deep fear of aban-

2. Douglas LaBier, *Modern Madness. The Emotional Fallout of Success.* Menlo Park, CA: Addison-Wesley, 1986.

donment by those "bigger than they upon whom they depend for basic life support." There is thus a deep feeling within such organizations of never being fully in control of one's own destiny. And they are right because they have traded self-control for protection. For this reason, we call such organizations Fearful Children.

Big Bullies and Fearful Children never really take or practice CM seriously, although they deceive themselves and the outside world by producing reams of manuals, documents, orders, rules, memos, which purport to establish the sincerity of their intentions. But such documents are nearly always a sham because their real energies are invested elsewhere; and in some sense, everyone connected with the organization knows it. In the case of Big Bullies, they are obsessed by the never-ending pursuit of power. In the case of Fearful Children, they are obsessed by the need to continually politic and kowtow to their "betters" in order to preserve their lifeline of support. Or better yet, everyone knows and doesn't know at the very same time, for both types engage in an incredible project of self-delusion. In this way, they protect themselves from having to really understand the consequences of their actions or their failures to act.

Finally, it is possible for both rationalizations one and eleven to operate within the same company. For instance, those at corporate headquarters may well believe in rationalization one since from their perspective they are the big, powerful corporation. At the same time, rationalizations ten and eleven as well as number one can also operate in the separate subdivisions or parts of the company since the various subdivisions are in effect protected, or at least have the illusion of it, by Big Daddy. However, companies which operate at the top by rationalization one often send a signal to those below that rationalization eleven is highly contingent upon their continued deference. Thus everyone below is sucked in both by the power and size of those above them and the fear that while they are protected by the organization, it has to be won continuously. It could be withdrawn arbitrarily at any time. Little wonder then why so many of the subdivisions under a Big Bully or Big Daddy spend an incredible amount of their time lobbying for support.

2. The Fallacy of Excellence
3. The Fallacy of Location/Geography
4. The Fallacy of Immunity/Limited Vulnerability

While certainly not identical with one, rationalizations two, three, and four in group one are offshoots of it nonetheless. In each case, the ardent desire is to find a special property of an organization that will guarantee protection from a major crisis. Thus, two expresses the misguided notion that "excellent/well-managed companies do not have crises"; four, that one doesn't have to worry about special kinds of crises, e.g., terrorism, because of one's geographical location; and five expresses the notion that one doesn't have to worry about certain kinds of crises, e.g., product tampering, because one is not in the business of producing food products. Each is wrong—dead wrong.

The Tylenol case is enough to dispel the notion that only poorly managed companies have major crises. Johnson & Johnson (J&J), the parent company of McNeil Pharmaceuticals, the makers of Tylenol, has been regarded for years as an enlightened, ethical, well-managed and -respected company. Unfortunately, this did not prevent J&J from experiencing a major crisis. Indeed, as we noted in the first chapter, a paradox that every successful company has to face in today's world is that its very success makes it a more tempting target.

The Salmon Rushdie case, i.e., the threats of terrorism directed against the publishers of *The Satanic Verses*, is enough to dispel the notion that there are still favored geographical locations in the world that exempt one from any kind of crisis, let alone terrorism. What is especially interesting about the Rushdie case is that one can well imagine the rolling of eyes that would have occurred if, say, a year prior to the incident one had approached the New York book publishers with the thought that they had better prepare for terrorism because of a popular book that they had published or were about to publish. One can imagine not only the rolling of eyes but the bursts of laughter that would have followed. And yet, if this case has anything to teach us, it should be the lesson that there are no protected regions of the globe in a world that is now totally interconnected by mass transportation and instant communications.

By the same token, it should be appreciated that all organizations are now subject to every known kind of crisis imaginable. Another one of the earliest findings of our research was that crises no longer occur singly and in isolation. Increasingly, crises occur in bunches or clusters as part of a chain reaction to an initial crisis. Consider, for instance, product tampering. While it is certainly true that a book publisher is not subject to product tampering by the injection of cyanide into its products (as author Umberto Eco's highly successful *The Name of The Rose* shows) so it is possible, in principle, to contaminate the pages of a book, that a person, by merely touching a wet finger to its pages and then placing the finger back on one's tongue, could die of poisoning. Over and over again, our research illustrates that one of the greatest sins in the area of CM is narrow, literal thinking. Every organization has to ask itself what is the *special form* of product tampering that could hurt it. Product tampering must not be taken literally. For example, tell the publishers of *Encyclopedia Britannica* that they were not subject to product tampering when someone broke into their computers, dumped in phony information, which was then printed out in the pages of the volumes. This is product tampering of the type that applies to all publishers. Or, tell the organizers of the Miss America Pageant a few years ago that when, unbeknownst to them, Vanessa Williams posed for sexually explicit photos, this also was not a form of product tampering. She essentially "tampered" with the supposedly good, clean, wholesome image that the organizers of the pageant wished to project. In today's environment, no organization can take it for granted that it will not be subject to any of these kinds of crises.

5. The Fallacy of "Business as Usual"
6. The Fallacy of Reactiveness
7. The Fallacy of Luxury

Even the best organizations have not learned all the necessary lessons. J&J rightly and legitimately has been touted as a corporate role model for how to deal with a major crisis. Thus, its CEO, James Burke, did not dodge the press, react with anger, or stonewall the problem. J&J even kept a faithful log of press inquiries so the company could get back with information when they had it. It responded quickly and effectively to the general American public and thus restored confidence both in it as a company and in Tylenol as a product. This response allowed J&J to bring it back to the market successfully, until the second crisis when they no longer felt that they could protect the drug adequately in its present form. They even withdrew the product from the market when they were advised *not* to by the FBI, thus earning the trust and confidence of the American public in that they were prepared to "do the right thing." Other organizations, such as Exxon, have now earned the contempt and general distrust of the American public.

However, no organization currently, at least those with which we are familiar, is a role model for all that we have learned and are continuing to learn about what needs to be done in the area of crisis management. J&J's top management believed that, prior to the two Tylenol crises, no special training would have helped them through their situation. Apparently they believe, even today, that prior to a crisis there are no special skills or training that can either be given or need to be given to a team of managers to prepare them. They believe that having a good management team in and of itself was enough. They believe that it was enough to respond reactively. Indeed, they believe this because in their view there wasn't much of anything one could do proactively before experiencing a major crisis. We disagree strongly.

There are two myths that arise perpetually in human affairs which constantly need to be beaten back. One is that there can be perfect or complete control of complex human situations. The other is that no control is possible at all.

It is true that every crisis involves an element of uniqueness (see rationalization number eighteen), but this does not mean that there are no general or generic features of crises or effective procedures for handling them whatsoever. All human situations involve an element of uniqueness. No two football players and no two football plays are ever exactly alike, but this doesn't keep coaches from conducting practices constantly so that their players can learn how to respond to generic situations. Similarly, no two battles are ever alike. But long ago generals realized that soldiers needed basic training *before* being sent into battle. While not perfect, basic training lowers substantially the physical and emotional casualties due to war. One of the purposes of basic training is *not* to avoid all casualties whatsoever, but precisely to free soldiers to think about the unique features of battle that cannot be planned for. The assumption is that soldiers will be freer to deal with the unique features that arise if the generic features have been planned for.

One of the worst consequences of any crisis is the emotional toll that is exacted, not only on the organization, but also on the individuals involved. It is generally not known or appreciated that a number of the executives associated with Tylenol had and continued to experience nightmares on the anniversary of the attacks. As part of our complex makeup, our emotional psyches are left with scars by the emotional trauma that accompany any major crisis. For example, NASA had to set up an emergency medical hotline when the seven astronauts were killed in the tragic explosion of the Space Shuttle Challenger. Upon returning home, a number of the employees who were associated with the mission were confronted by the seemingly innocent question from their children: "Mommy, Daddy, were you responsible for killing the astronauts?" Even under the best of circumstances, untrained human beings cannot cope with such questions. As a result, a number of NASA's employees experienced severe emotional distress.

Crises involve a large number of rationalizations, unstated as well as stated. One of the biggest unstated rationalizations, and for this very reason one that we have not heard expressed, but one which operates nonetheless, is: "We will not suffer an emotional trauma or experience severe emotional reactions as the result of a major crisis." This assumption is entirely false. One of the biggest reasons why it is difficult for any company to go back and instigate a successful CM program following a major crisis is that the very basic training that would prepare it for a new crisis will necessarily open old traumatic wounds that have not been fully dealt with and have not had the proper time to heal. As a result, not just J&J, but countless other organizations which have experienced a crisis prefer instead to avoid the serious debriefing of how they handled it financially, physically, and emotionally. This is a shame, for a review, conducted not for the purpose of blaming people or finding scapegoats, would help the company prepare better for the future. Another unspoken assumption or rationalization is: "That which is not discussed or talked about will not only go away but have no effect upon the organization." This rationalization like all the others that we have encountered is also unfortunately false and can exert a damaging effect upon any organization.

Without a doubt, one of the most difficult issues in the whole area of CM is the amount of money or finances that should be allocated to the preparation for crises. If there is any area in which the field of crisis management is currently weak, then this is certainly it. We just do not have available at this time the data that would allow us to conduct a systematic and thorough "cost benefit" analysis of how much money an organization should spend on crisis management. However, some indications are emerging as to how one ought to go about thinking about this matter. For instance, prior to the fire that disrupted a major telephone switching station of Illinois Bell in the Chicago area, one company spent $600,000 backing up its extensive telecommunications and computer facilities in the case of such an eventuality. Six hundred thousand dollars is certainly a great deal of money. However, as a result of the $600,000, the company did *not* lose $20 million in business as a result of the fire. From this standpoint 3 percent (or $600,000) is a wise investment on $20 million. Further, the company was able to make a significant increase in its share of the market since it was able to conduct business while its competitors were not.

But there is an even more important point about cost. In the late 1980s, *Business Week*[3] ran an article dealing with the new kinds of accounting procedures that are needed in the global information age. It made the exceedingly important point that in today's world it is no longer proper accounting procedure merely to evaluate the cost of computers and telecommunications in terms of their initial purchase and maintenance costs. From PCs to FAX machines, modern computers and telecommunications equipment are so integral to the conduct of literally every business that no organization can stay in business for long without them. The question of cost is akin to asking what is the proper cost human beings ought to put on the blood that circulates in their bodies or on the oxygen they breathe constantly. The true cost of computers and telecommunications can no longer be equated with their initial purchase or maintenance costs but rather with the cost of going out of business if the machines are unable to function.

The proper way to think about CM is not as insurance or a luxury that one indulges in if one has the time and the money to spend. Rather, CM cannot really be separated from the day-to-day ongoing conduct of one's business. CM is central to the conduct of everyday business in that a major crisis can seriously disrail any business. This does not mean, as rationalization number five would have us believe, that CM does not involve special training or skills. Rather, the kinds of skills, which we discuss in another chapter, need to become part of the new skills that are necessary to compete in the global economy.

19. Crises Are Not Solely Negative in Their Impacts

One of the most persistent myths about crises is that they are solely negative in their impacts both on individuals and organizations. Given what we have just gotten through saying in the preceding sec-

3. Otis Port, Resa King, William J. Hampton, "How the New Math of Productivity Adds Up," *Business Week*, June 6, 1988, pp. 103-115.

tion, one can well understand why many believe this. And indeed, for the most part the impacts are negative. As we have continually stressed, crises exact a severe financial, physical, and emotional toll on both individuals and organizations. However, there are some aspects of crises which strangely enough turn out to be positive, although one wished that there were other ways of reaping such benefits. If one talks to enough top executives and CEOs, a strange and unexpected benefit emerges. Many a CEO will say something along the following lines:

Although I didn't realize it at the time, and I'm not sure I would have us go through it again, it turned out that there was some exceedingly positive benefits to the crisis we experienced. For one, it forced us to make some longstanding changes that I'd unsuccessfully been trying to get through our organization for years. For example, I have been trying to get two different departments to merge since what each of them was doing was so obviously and heavily dependent upon the other. They avoided merging because of all kinds of political turf battles. One thing you find out during the heat of a crisis is that it forces you to cross over set organizational boundaries that don't make much sense for today's world.

If a crisis can bring out the worst in some people, then it generally brought out the best in all of us. I found out that this is pretty much the opinion of other CEOs and top executives with whom I have talked. Our people were more than willing to cooperate, to spend hours working way beyond their normal job duties.

Some of our competitors even came to our help by giving us space and allowing us to use their telephones. In short, everyone cooperated with us. Even our suppliers were great. We got endless calls from even people just off the street asking how they could help us.

In many ways, I and others around here find ourselves asking the same question over and over again, "How can we get the same great behavior, the cooperation, the high energy, the deep participation and true involvement now that our crisis has passed?" In many ways, the crisis that occurred was the best thing that happened to us for years. One of the worst things about a crisis is something we found out after it had passed. People slide back into their old routines. When I think about it, we became almost like a Japanese organization. Everyone gave 110 percent and didn't care about petty titles and job descriptions and so on.

Again, the biggest benefit was that our crisis forced us to make some permanent changes in our organization. What really bothers me is that we've begun to slide back into complacency. Do we need a crisis a month, once a year to keep us on the right track? Do we need a crisis daily to get our attention to see that we have to be continually adaptive to a new environment? Is crisis the only way to get a big, unwieldy organization, and we're as good an example as any, to change? But then to paraphrase, nothing focuses and concentrates our energies as does a crisis, especially one that threatens your very existence!

CONCLUDING REMARKS

The rationalizations we have observed in this chapter unfortunately are not the complete or final word. New ones are continually emerging. We make no pretences about our having captured them all.

The rationalizations that we have discussed in this chapter were among the very first signs we observed of what made an organization Crisis Prone versus Crisis Prepared. Indeed, we first observed the rationalizations we write about in this chapter before we observed the games that individuals play. In many cases, the executives we interviewed disagreed strongly and vehemently with the rationalizations their organizations espouse. The rationalizations did not necessarily express how they felt personally or what they believed. Rather, they expressed the general thought patterns, character, or culture of their organization. In many cases, the individual games they played that we discussed earlier were the direct result of the games their organizations played.

It is tempting to view the rationalizations merely as fragmented, isolated expressions of corporate character. This is wrong. The rationalizations are indicative of the games that are played at the level of the whole organization. To see this, we have grouped in Table 2 most of the rationalizations in Table 1 under those games that are played at the level of the organization.

Table 2
Games That Are Played at The Level of the Whole Organization

Bigger Is Better	The Magician or Illusion	Excellence	Buffering
Our Size Will Protect Us	Crises Do Not Require Special Procedures	Excellent, Well-Managed Companies Do Not Have Crises	Our Special Location Will Protect Us
	Crisis Management or Crisis Prevention Is A Luxury	We Are A Team That Will Function Well During A Crisis	Certain Crises Only Happen To Others
	If A Major Crisis Happens, Someone Else Will Rescue Us		Crises Do Not Require Special Procedures
	The Environment Is Benign, or, We Can Effectively Buffer Ourselves From The Environment		Crisis Managment Is Someone Else's Responsibility
	It's Not A Crisis If It Doesn't Happen To Or Hurt Us		The Environment Is Benign, or, We Can Effectively Buffer Ourselves From The Environment
	Most Crises Turn Out Not To Be Very Important		Nothing New Has Really Occurred That Warrants Change
	It's Enough To Throw Technical And Financial Quick Fixes At A Problem		It's Not A Crisis If It Doesn't Happen To Or Hurt Us
	Crisis Management Is Like An Insurance Policy; You Only Need To Buy So Much		Most Crises Turn Out Not To Be Very Important
	We Are Tough Enough To React To A Crisis In An Objective And Rational Manner		Each Crisis Is So Unique That It Is Not Possible To Prepare For Them
			Crises Are Isolated
			The Only Important Thing In Crisis Management Is To Make Sure That Our Internal Operations Stay Intact

Technophilia	Image	Resourcism	Blaming	Poor Me
Most, If Not All, Crises Have A Technical Solution	We Know How To Manipulate The Media	Crime/Murder Is Just A Cost Of Doing Business	Employees Who Bring Bad News Deserve To Be Punished	If A Major Crisis Happens, Someone Else Will Rescue Us
It's Enough To Throw Technical And Financial Quick-Fixes At A Problem				
In A Crisis Situation, We Just Need To Refer To The Emergency Procedures We've Laid Out In Our Crisis Manuals				

Razor's Edge	Be Nice To People	Buddies	Fragmentation
Desirable Business Ends Justify The Taking of High-Risk Means	Only Executives Need To Be Aware Of Our Crisis Plans; Why Scare Our Employees Or Members Of The Community?	Only Executives Need To Be Aware Of Our Crisis Plans; Why Scare Our Employees Or Members Of The Community	Crisis Management Is Someone Else's Responsibility
Me Before Anyone			The Environment Is Benign, or, We Can Effectively Buffer Ourselves From The Environment
The Only Important Thing In Crisis Management Is To Make Sure That Our Internal Operations Stay Intact			It's Not A Crisis If It Doesn't Happen To Or Hurt Us
			Most Crises Turn Out Not To Be Very Important
			Crises Are Isolated

From Table 2 it can be seen that organizations themselves play essentially the same games that individuals play. However, because this finding or conclusion is so important as well as complex, it needs to be given some interpretation. In Chapters 3 and 4, we described essentially the games that individuals play on themselves, against themselves, as well as against others, and even against the organization as a whole. They engage in such games because of defects that they bring with them to the organization, defects that are often magnified by the nature of the organization itself. In this chapter, we have attempted to describe those games and rationalizations that organizations play against the outside world or environment. What we have not described is a whole host of other games that organizations play toward all of their members. For example, one of the most prevalent organizational games played toward their top members is that of Got You. This game is particularly insidious. In essence, the game is one of entrapment. Once one has worked for an organization long enough and presumably is earning a great deal of money, the person is as much trapped by the organization as he or she is rewarded by it. Many organizations, subtly of course, play the game of, "Now that I own you, I can abuse you, if not humiliate you." As important as such games are, we have deliberately chosen not to explore them in this chapter, not because they are not significant but because the games that are revealed through rationalizations are less apparent.

Chapter 6

How Healthy Companies Break Out of Dangerous Games, and Conversely, How Unhealthy Companies Stay Trapped

. . . Modern western men, in contrast with Shakespeare's heroes . . . are required to present a facade of coolness, lack of excitement, even boredom, to express emotion only rarely and then for relatively trivial events, such as sporting occasions, where the emotions expressed are acknowledged to be dramatized and so are not taken entirely seriously. Thus, women in our society form the main group allowed or even expected to feel emotion. A woman may cry in the face of disaster, and a man of color may gesticulate, but a white man merely sets his jaw.

White men's control of their emotional expression may go to the extremes of repressing their emotions, failing to develop emotionally, or even losing the capacity to experience many emotions. Not uncommonly, these men are unable to identify what they are feeling, and even they may be surprised, on occasion, by their own apparent lack of emotional response to a situation, such as a death, where emotional reaction is perceived appropriate. In some married couples, the wife implicitly is assigned the job of feeling emotion for both of them. White college-educated men increasingly enter therapy in order to learn how to "get in touch with" their emotions, a project other men may ridicule as weakness. In therapeutic situations, men may learn that they are just as emotional as women but less adept at identifying their own or others' emotions. In consequence, their emotional development may be relatively rudimentary; this may lead to moral rigidity or insensitivity. Paradoxically, men's lacking awareness of their own emotional responses frequently results in their being more influenced by emotions rather than less.

Alison M. Jaggar,
"Love and Knowledge: Emotion in
Feminist Epistemology,"
in Ann Garry and Marilyn Pearsall (Eds.),
*Women, Knowledge, and Reality:
Explorations in Feminist Philosophy*,
Unwin Hyman, Boston, 1989, p. 142

One of the most powerful things that happens during a crisis is the collapse of an organization's fundamental belief system—its most cherished beliefs about itself and its environment. This phenomenon is so important that we want to illustrate it in terms of a brief case with which the first author was recently involved.

One of the country's major zoos was faced with a potential crisis of alleged animal abuse. In particular, it was charged with abusing the elephants under its care. Somehow or another the organization weathered the crisis in that it "passed over." However, while this zoo was in the midst of the crisis, there was a great deal of concern as to what effect this would have on its reputation. Also, whether this would have an adverse effect on short-term donations from the community upon which it depended for support, not to mention more critical losses that would accrue if its good reputation were damaged permanently.

A few months after the crisis had simmered down, Mitroff was called in to review what had happened to see if there were any critical lessons that could be learned from it. By way of an introduction, he gave a general lecture on crisis management. In addition, he helped the organization accomplish something which few rarely do: go back and see what their belief system was prior to the crisis and how the crisis had damaged that system almost fatally.

It took a good couple of hours but slowly and surely, thirty or so of the major assumptions that the organization had made about itself and the outside world prior to the crisis emerged. Literally every one of these assumptions had been proven wrong or invalid by the crisis situation.

This is not an easy exercise to accomplish, not because it is difficult intellectually, but because it is taxing emotionally. People have to admit to themselves and in front of others that some of the things that they have long believed about their organization are no longer true, if indeed they ever had been. In effect, they have to challenge some of their most fundamental beliefs about the world, beliefs which rarely surface because they are taken for granted.

At the end of the day, the thirty or so erroneous beliefs were put up on a flipchart for all to see. It became readily apparent to everyone that they fell into three major groups consisting of about ten assumptions per cluster. Each of the clusters was so distinct that an interesting portrait emerged not only of this organization, but of a lot of organizations, especially technical ones, and even those which provide public service.

The first cluster of ten assumptions was judged most important, and which, prior to the crisis, the organization believed possessed a "high degree of truth." In one way or another, all ten of the assumptions in this group expressed the fact that this organization truly believed that its great scientific standing lent credibility to whatever it said. If it said that they had not abused elephants, then it was certain that the *outside world* would believe it as well. As this organization learned painfully, and in many cases it is still in need of learning, the outside world is not composed of scientists. Those who go to zoos do not do so because they are scientists but because they like animals. While it is absolutely *necessary* for the zoo to maintain its high credibility and standing with the scientific community, this is *not sufficient* when it comes to gaining the general public's trust and confidence.

Prior to the crisis, a second set of assumptions had also been judged to be fairly critical, although with a far less degree of certainty with regard to their truth than the first set. The second group of ten assumptions pertained in one way or another to the fact that the organization truly believed that its own employees would not sabotage or betray it. And yet, it was precisely the zoo's own employees that had first released the information to the press of the various allegations of animal abuse by coworkers.

Finally, the remaining set of assumptions referred to the presumed belief that if a crisis happened, then the zoo's "sister" organizations would naturally rush to its defense. In the past, the zoo had worked closely with the Humane Society and other organizations on projects such as the protection of animals. The zoo falsely assumed that in its hour of need these organizations would close ranks.

This organization was truly shocked to find that during the heat of its crisis, *nearly every single one of its fundamental beliefs about itself and the outside world were rendered almost totally invalid!* Overnight, their beliefs collapsed almost entirely. And yet, if a major crisis has anything to teach us, it tells us that this is precisely what happens. A major crisis doesn't just challenge or destroy one or two critical beliefs. It threatens and challenges every one of them. We cannot overemphasize this. There is little doubt that almost any organization can survive if merely one or two of its fundamental beliefs about itself and the world are challenged. But it is truly a crisis in the most fundamental existential sense of the term when every one of the beliefs that it has used to give meaning and order to its world has been challenged and rendered invalid by outside events. This is particularly true if the organization itself is responsible for causing a crisis of unparalleled dimensions.

In a similar fashion, if a major crisis challenges the belief system of an organization, then it also challenges the personal belief systems of many of the individuals that are connected with the organization. A major crisis is an existential crisis not only for the organization as a whole, but also for many of the individuals connected with it, such as the families of employees.

Although we have not been able to talk directly to people inside of Exxon, from what we have read and from those we've spoken to in the oil industry, it is clear that Exxon was operating under a host of false, if not faulty, beliefs. The Exxon Valdez crisis revealed that the following were *all invalid*:

(1) that Exxon and the state of Alaska were prepared for a crisis of the magnitude that occurred,

(2) that the proper cleanup equipment was actually there and in good operating order,

(3) that crews had been well trained and well practiced in the event of such a spill,

(4) that the proper procedures for a spill of the magnitude encountered would be followed, notwithstanding their viability,

(5) that the weather would be benign,

(6) that everyone truly knew his role and what to do,

(7) that the information and communication lines of the company were open so that different divisions could get the proper trained personnel to the spot and help in the cleanup.

Fortunately, even in the rather depressing area of CM, there exist examples that not only are humorous but also show, nonetheless, the extremely critical role that assumptions play. The late Ray Kroc, founder of McDonald's, provides an excellent example.

At one point McDonald's was faced with the rumor that it had put worms in its hamburger. Ray Kroc flew down to the region of the country in which this was supposed to have happened and went on TV to explain the situation. He did it in a way that should serve as a model for all organizations, provided they have a spokesman with Kroc's appealing personality and the data to show that they are right.

Kroc explained in a homespun fashion: "Because of our size, McDonald's buys a lot of hamburger. In fact, we're able to buy the very best for about only 75 cents a pound. Now folks, you may not realize this, but worms cost $3.00 a pound. Think about it for a second! Would we be so dumb as to put worms in our hamburger when it costs so much more?"

Aside from the obvious humor in Kroc's logic, look at what he did so effectively. The inherent assumption on the part of the public before they heard Kroc was that hamburger was expensive and worms were free! What Kroc did was to show that just the reverse was true: worms were expensive and hamburger was relatively cheap! In one fell swoop, Kroc was able to pull the entire underpinnings out from the argument that McDonald's was engaging in a disgusting act by turning the assumptions of the case on their heads. If the reversal of assumptions thus often can prove disastrous for an organization, then they can also prove to be extremely helpful if the reversal of assumptions is used knowingly and effectively by the right person. The major point is that the surfacing, critique, and challenging of assumptions is one of the most critical activities that anyone who wishes to stay in business and to stay alive in a complex environment needs to do.

THE FAILURE OF SUCCESS:
THE CASE OF THE U.S. AUTO INDUSTRY

We want to discuss another example that shows how critical are the assumptions that an organization or industry makes about itself. In particular, we want to give two slightly different treatments of the critical assumptions that underlay the strategies of the U.S. automobile industry. The first set comes primarily from a number of scholarly books on the history of the industry in general.[1] The second comes from a study that was done of General Motors in particular.[2] Both studies indicate that the life cycle of the automobile industry's critical premises was no more than sixty years at best. From roughly 1910 to 1970, the assumptions directing the industry not only were valid, but made for the overwhelming success of one of the most effective industries the world has ever known. But then almost overnight, in the span of some five to ten years, the American automobile industry virtually collapsed. It became invalid and so out of touch with reality that it almost went down the tubes—for good.

Table 1 shows what we refer to as the "Unwritten Rules of the American Automobile Industry." Notice that we have listed the rules in two columns. The first shows our interpretations of the more scholarly wording of the assumptions which we have listed in the second.

As you look down the list, you can see that the assumptions are so intertwined with technological, human, social, and organizational factors that it's literally impossible to say where one factor clearly leaves off and another begins. In effect, the entire list constitutes a complete social contract for running the automobile business. In one way or another, all of them assume that nearly everyone connected with the system had no need for more than a fragmented, compartmentalized understanding of the business. Thus, Table 1 provides testimony to the long history of the Fragmentation game played by the U.S. auto industry as a whole.

Among many other things, it was also assumed that customer preferences were well understood and that customers really didn't want very sophisticated cars. All of these things may appear stupid to us now, but they weren't for a long time, almost sixty years.

The failure of the automobile industry was the failure to see that when these assumptions began to change, the industry needed to base its practices on new assumptions. The greatest difficulty here is that when a set of rules makes sense for so long, it's almost impossible to

1. See for instance P. R. Lawrence and D. Dyer, *Renewing American Industry*, New York: Free Press, 1983.
2. Jim O'Toole, "Declining Innovation: The Failure of Success. A Summary Report of the Seventh Twenty Year Forecast Project," Center for Futures Research, Graduate School of Business, University of Southern California, 1983.

TABLE 1
The Unwritten Rules of the American Automobile Industry

STRAIGHT TALK	PROFESSIONAL TALK
1. An easy, short childhood is the best preparation for adulthood and maturity.	It was a distinct advantage that by about 1930 the modern car industry was firmly established, its competitive practies well understood, its major product design features firmly locked into place, etc.
2. We are stable now and forever-more; the broader world is stable.	The competitive dynamics and basic business of automobile production is essentially stable and well known.
3. "They love us" (i.e., our products); they're loyal, won't switch; we can take them for granted; we can assume consumer stability.	The tastes of U.S. car buyers are standardized and stable; thus, except for yearly styling changes, we do not have to make radical or substantial changes in our product. U.S. car buyers will not demand a new type of car that we have never built in large volume before.
4. Nothing new will be invented that will radically shake up our product; essentially, we know it all; the stability of car technology can be taken for granted.	The design/production of future cars will not require fundamental new manufacturing processes or technologies.
5. Our focus need not be broader than the driver; a restricted focus of innovation can be assumed.	Innovations relating to driver comfort are more important than fundamental technical innovations in the basic product.
6. Don't change until forced to; resist, deny change; put your major energies into denial and resistance.	We can succeed by not spending money on fundamental innovations until forced to by governmental regulatory agencies, foreign competition, consumers, etc.
7. Get your priorities wrong; innovation can take a backseat to efficiency.	Because of GM's dominant industry strategy (under A. P. Sloan), based on clever marketing to different demographic segments of the population and frequent style changes, technical innovation was subordinated to efficiency in production, i.e., efficiency is more important than innovation.

TABLE 1 (Continued)
The Unwritten Rules of the American Automobile Industry

STRAIGHT TALK	PROFESSIONAL TALK
8. Keep getting your priorities wrong; good labor relations can take a backseat to efficiency.	Efficiency in production is more important than good labor relations; good labor relations are not important to efficiency.
9. We're so big and powerful, smug and secure that we can shut out the whole world; we can charge and pass on anything we want to our customers. So what if we're arrogant?	Foreign competition will never be significant; therefore, U.S. car makers will not be prevented from passing the higher costs of production necessary to keep up with the competition on to consumers.
10. Since we don't need much innovation, we can finance whatever we want to.	The capital and debt capacity required to finance whatever innovations are required will be readily available.
11. Managers don't need challenge in their work; the restricted focus/nature of managerial work can be assumed.	As the business of car making became well understood, not only did managerial work become routine, but it was desirable that it did so. The challenge of managerial work was not necessary to the long-term success of the industry.
12. If you want to get tunnel vision, then you have to reward it. We are masters at creating a system for producing managerial myopia.	An extremely handsome bonus system that rewards top management for short-term thinking is not hazardous to the long-term interests of the entire industry.
13. Workers don't need challenge in their jobs; the restricted focus/nature of all jobs can be assumed.	Workers are willing to trade money for challenge in their jobs.
14. Keep everyone small-minded and uninvolved.	It is not necessary to engage most employees in the larger purposes of the business.
15. Don't rock the boat, don't bite the hand that feeds you; these rules pertain to the unwritten culture of the industry.	It is not in the interest of top managers to tamper with the system that has promoted them. It is not necessary for top management to look at the big or whole picture.

TABLE 1 (Continued)
The Unwritten Rules of the American Automobile Industry

STRAIGHT TALK	PROFESSIONAL TALK
16. We don't need constant informal parties as they do in Silicon Valley.	It is not necessary to foster an industry-wide culture of innovation, intense competition between companies, informal sharing of information, entrepreneurism, and the intense cycling of executives between firms.
17. We've discovered *the* principles of organization for all time.	Not only is the organizational structure of U.S. car makers appropriate for its time, if not all time, but it is well suited to responding to changing governmental policies, consumer tastes, and foreign competition.
18. No one, including ourselves, can teach us anything about good organization; we resist learning anything even from ourselves.	Despite GM's great success due to its early organizational structure under Alfred P. Sloan, Ford was correct to resist the professionalization of its upper management for so long, and Chrysler was correct to resist adopting GM's structure of high differentiation and high integration. In other words, U.S. car makers had nothing significant to learn from one another regarding the design of their respective organizational structures.

change those rules because they begin to take on the character of eternal truths.

The moral is: *the U.S. auto industry didn't fail because it was a failure from day one but because it was a success for so long and took its success for granted!* The industry thought it had found the magic formula for eternal success when all it had found was a particular set of conditions that were only good for a limited period of time.

We repeat: The failure of the U.S. auto industry is not the "failure of failure"; instead, it is the "failure of success." Like most industries, instead of changing when it needed to—and in the best of all possible circumstances, anticipating changes—it did even more of the same: It reinforced its old assumptions even more.

Now look at Table 2, which lists the particular set of assumptions that pertain specifically to GM. The first column outlines the generic

TABLE 2
General Motors: Assumptions and Counter-Assumptions

GENERIC ISSUES	OLD OPERATING ASSUMPTIONS	NEW OPERATING ASSUMPTIONS
1. What business are we basically in? Who has basic control of the organization?	1. GM is in the business of making money, not cars. (The accounting and finance people took over control of the organization after the industry passed its start-up phase, which was run by people who wanted to make cars.)	1. GM is primarily in the business of making quality cars, not money. Any organization that forgets its purpose for going into business in the first place will not achieve one of its fundamental financial objectives. (The engineers and the accounting/finance people should share control.)
2. What must our posture toward innovation be?	2. Success comes not from technological leadership but from having the resources to quickly adopt innovations successfully introduced by others.	2. We cannot give up technological leadership in a world that is more competitive than ever. We no longer have the luxury of time in a more complex environment.
3. How does the customer view our product?	3. Cars are primarily status symbols. Styling is therefore more important than quality to buyers who are, after all, going to trade up every other year.	3. Quality and styling are equally important in a more competitive market where even the cheapest car is expensive by past standards and where the competition is able to produce well-crafted and stylish products.

TABLE 2 (Continued)
General Motors: Assumptions and Counter-Assumptions

GENERIC ISSUES	OLD OPERATING ASSUMPTIONS	NEW OPERATING ASSUMPTIONS
4. How much control do we actually have over our outside environment? How much can we really insulate ourselves from it?	4. The American car market is isolated from the rest of the world. Foreign competitors will never gain more than 15% of the domestic market.	4. The American car market will never be as isolated from the rest of the world as it once was. Foreign competition is here to stay, and it will always be significant.
5. What are the basic resources this organization needs in order to do business, and how available will they be in the future?	5. Energy will always be cheap and abundant.	5. Energy will never again be cheap or abundant, even though it may be held artificially low for what seems like an indefinite period of time; it will fluctuate enormously.
6. What skills and education of personnel do we need to presume in order to do business?	6. Workers do not have an important impact on productivity or product quality.	6. Even with automation, worker attitudes and skills at all levels are more important than ever.
7. How isolated are we from the shifting concerns of our customers?	7. The consumer movement does not represent a significant portion [of] the American public.	7. Given the rising costs of all products and the increasing concern with the environment, there will continue to be some organizations that will represent these concerns. Any organization that ignores them is dangerously deluding itself.

TABLE 2 (Continued)
General Motors: Assumptions and Counter-Assumptions

GENERIC ISSUES	OLD OPERATING ASSUMPTIONS	NEW OPERATING ASSUMPTIONS
8. What is our attitude toward the government? Who do we perceive to be our natural enemies, our allies; why?	8. The government is the enemy. It must be fought tooth and nail every inch of the way.	8. The government is a significant factor in the environment, and as such it must be dealt with whether one likes it or not. It is too easy to blame others for our problems.
9. Which types of controls are appropriate?	9. Strict, centralized financial controls are the secret to good administration.	9. Compulsive financial controls arc thc cause and effect of bad administration. There is all the difference in the world between a financial system that *controls* an organization and one that *enables* it to do what it wants to and should do.
10. How closed off is our organization to new ideas from the outside? How open, how trusting are we? What's our organizational culture like?	10. Managers should be developed from the inside.	10. The culture of an organization should be continually assessed to ensure that it has not become a closed system resistant to new ideas.

set of issues that GM, like all organizations, had to manage. The middle one describes the old operating assumptions. In many ways, they merely repeat the assumptions contained in Table 1. We have listed them again in order to lay out the new operating assumptions that we believe GM, as well as every member of the automobile industry, now has to abide by.

One of the key points of this discussion is that the top management of an organization is the prime keeper and formulator of the principal assumptions that support everything the organization does. Assumptions are thus so important that we can summarize their importance in a kind of formula: *The quality of a company's assumptions multiplied by the quality of its production processes equals the quality of its performance times the quality of its delivered products.* As an "equation," it looks like this:

Quality of a company's assumptions	×	Quality of its production processes	=	Quality of its performance as a firm	×	Quality of its delivered products

One needs quality at every point along the entire process in order to get quality at the end. We can't separate any of the factors in this equation. One is tempted to call the quality of a company's assumptions the "soft" part of management and the quality of a firm's production processes the "hard" part, but we don't think the words "hard" and "soft" really make sense in today's world. We would rather say that we are dealing with the importance of one set of factors times the importance of another set of factors which equals importance squared; and importance squared equals something highly critical. It doesn't matter whether a factor is "hard" or "soft" as long as it's important. It's importance that counts, not the terms or the outmoded labels "hardness" or "softness." We are stressing this because we think far too many people overemphasize the importance of one factor or another when it's really both that count. And if both count equally, it doesn't really matter what one calls the factors except that too many otherwise intelligent people get misdirected by inappropriate and simpleminded labels.

What good is the distinction "soft" versus "hard" if every so-called "hard" factor depends upon a set of "soft" assumptions? Did the Space Shuttle Challenger blow up because of the failure of the "hard" O-ring (i.e., technology) or because of the "soft" communications and organizational breakdown (i.e., human factors)? It failed because of both. That's why the distinction is irrelevant at best and stupid and misleading at worst. The distinction diverts us from recognizing that both are important no matter what they're called.

Look at the right side of the equation. The quality of performance means not only how well an organization does on "the bottom line" but how well its people feel about the organization. How well the organization communicates and provides the right information to the right people is critical to achieving quality in its final delivered products.

HOW HEALTHY COMPANIES BREAK OUT OF DANGEROUS GAMES

As we stated in the previous chapter, we cannot mention the names of the organizations that we have surveyed. However, we can say almost unequivocally that in every case where we have encountered an organization that we would label as either "healthy" or as Crisis Prepared, we have found an organization that was dynamic and flexible enough not only to know but also to challenge its most fundamental assumptions. While there are a number of things that make an organization healthy, certainly assumption-challenging is high on the list.

In the September-October 1989 issue of the *Harvard Business Review*, there was a very short article by Ricardo Semler, president of a diversified manufacturing company called Semco, one of "Brazil's fastest-growing companies with a profit margin in 1988 of 10 percent on sales of $37 million."[3] What is important about the article is that in a relatively short period of time before it was written, Semco was literally on the point of collapse. More significant, however, are the truly radical sets of actions on which Semco embarked in order to turn its situation around. We are convinced that knowingly or not Semco engaged in a series of actions that fundamentally broke the back of every one of the crises or "Busy-ness" games. For this reason, it is important to spell out the set of actions or principles in which Semco engaged in order to restructure, redesign, and remotivate itself so that everyone connected with it could truly turn to the primary business at hand: producing quality products that would generate handsome profits for the company and for its community. In each case, Semco's actions were predicated on challenging and reversing a major taken-for-granted principle of management. In order to see this, let us briefly list the rules by which Semco governs itself:

1. In principle, everyone in the organization has access to the company's books, i.e., financial records and plans.

---

3. Ricardo Semler, "Managing Without Managers, How One Unorthodox Company Makes Money by Avoiding Decisions, Rules, and Executive Authority," *Harvard Business Review*, September-October 1989, pp. 76-83.

2. Everyone including workers set his or her own working hours.
   a. Thus, Semco has eliminated time clocks entirely.
3. There is company-wide voting on many important corporate decisions; for example: whether to purchase a plant or a business.
   a. Even in the case where Mr. Semler disagreed with an important corporate decision, but the employees voted to go ahead, the decision was made to go ahead, thus putting the notion of participatory management to a true test.
4. Management sets its own salaries and bonuses.
5. Semco is organized such that there is no unit larger than 150 people. This reflects the strong belief that mankind was not psychologically made to work in large impersonal groups; for most of history people have existed in small clans.
6. There are four titles composing no more than three layers of management in the company. At the top the president and top management are not known as such, but rather as "counselors."
   a. The next layer down consists of the heads of the eight major operating divisions known as partners. Below them are associates and coordinators at the same level.
   b. It is Semco's firm belief that the typical pyramidal structure of most organizations consisting of countless managers and their titles constitutes one of the biggest obstacles to participatory management.
   c. In order to break out of the trap in which most organizations find themselves, and to make participatory management into reality, one has to break out of the traditional structure that governs most organizations.
   d. In the language of this book, one has to have the right kind of structure in order to break out of the various games in which most organizations find themselves trapped.
7. Associates often make higher salaries than those at the upper levels, thus reflecting the principle that one does not have to enter the management line in order to make more money.

8. Periodically the employees are asked what it would take for them to strike or to quit.
9. Workers not only participate in the management of the organization but, more importantly, they participate in its design.
   a. For example, the workers themselves hired one of Brazil's leading architects to produce the layout for a flexible manufacturing system.
   b. As a result, Semco's "president" often feels like the plant belongs more to the employees than it does to him; in many ways he feels like a "guest" when walking into the plant.
10. One of the most important principles of all is Semco's fundamental belief that "we hire adults and treat them like adults."
11. As a result, Semco has abolished most norms, rules, manuals, and regulations, reflecting its belief that most of them are poppycock to begin with.
12. Instead, Semco runs itself through "common sense."
   a. It is also believed that common sense requires a touch of civil disobedience; one has to free the inherent Thoreaus and Tom Paines who are walking around.
   b. For Semco, civil disobedience is *not* a sign of revolution, but instead, a clear indication of common sense at work.
   c. As a result, it has replaced most of its prior nitpicking regulations with a strong dose of common sense.
   d. Another way to put it is to say that Semco places its employees in "the demanding position of using their own judgment."
   e. As a consequence, Semco has no dress code, reflecting the fact that dress has very little effect on performance and to believe it does is nonsense.
13. Semco has scrapped most of its prior travel expense reporting schemes which occupied far too much time and energy.
   a. Semco makes the strong assumption that if it can't trust its people in filling out travel expense report forms, how can they represent the company overseas when far more is at stake?
14. Adhering to its policy of hiring adults and then wishing to

treat them as adults, it has refused to humiliate the 97 percent of its employees who are law-abiding in order to get its hands on the occasional thief.

    a. The principle that Semco hires adults and wishes to treat them as such cannot be overemphasized; Semco puts it as follows: "On the outside people vote and make countless important decisions every day which affect not only them but the life of the nation. Why then do we expect them to put aside their adultlike behaviors and become like a child when they come in the factory doors?"

15. Semco insists on job rotation every two to five years to prevent boredom.

    a. Thus, it is vitally important to see that Semco has explicitly built in, i.e., not left to chance, a structural mechanism that explicitly facilitates breaking out of so many of the games that we have encountered previously that lead to "busy-ness" for its own sake.

16. Many of the employees who are hired in the beginning have no job description at all. They can do anything they want for up to a period of a year and a half as long as they are exposed to twelve different areas in the corporation.

17. Management forms groups into which workers fit but the work groups themselves appoint their own leaders.

    a. Thus, there is indeed a structure to Semco, but it is not one that is imposed completely from above.

18. Finally, Semco believes deeply in profit sharing and further that profit sharing is not a socialist invention but rather a capitalist one. Indeed, other than that of rewarding employees financially for a job well done, what other tool is as motivating?

CONCLUDING REMARKS

The moral of the Semco story is certainly not that all healthy companies are the same or that they necessarily need to restructure themselves as radically or as thoroughly as Semco has. Rather, the moral is that on every front and dimension of our existence it is no longer "business as usual."[4] Crisis-Prepared organizations realize this instinctively. Perhaps this is why they are constantly surfacing and testing their most cherished beliefs and assumptions with regard to their continued validity. Not only are they not afraid to critique their fundamental beliefs, but everyone connected with the organization is continually encouraged to do so. Furthermore, they realize that the fundamental premises from which they operate are so important that their surfacing and their challenging cannot be left to chance. As a result, they even sponsor company-wide internal workshops or colloquia to continually challenge, and only after this has been done, reaffirm their company credo, founding vision, as well as their basic operating principles. Only in this way do they believe that they can continue to remain viable.[5]

Because the uncovering and challenging of assumptions is so important, we want to illustrate this process even further in the next chapter.

4. Ian I. Mitroff, *Business Not as Usual, Rethinking Our Individual, Corporate, and Industrial Strategies for Global Competition*. San Francisco: Jossey-Bass, 1988.
5. For a detailed treatment on how to help companies challenge and break the pattern of their old assumptions, see Richard O. Mason and Ian I. Mitroff, *Challenging Strategic Planning Assumptions*. New York: John Wiley & Sons, 1981; see also Ian I. Mitroff, *Break-Away Thinking. How to Challenge Your Business Assumptions (And Why You Should)*. New York: John Wiley & Sons, 1988.

Chapter 7

Management by Nosing Around

A comforting but false idea about institutional thinking has gained some recent currency. This is the notion that institutions just do the routine, low-level, day-to-day thinking. Andrew Schotter, who has so well described institutions as machines for thinking, believes that the minor decisions get off-loaded for institutional processing, while the mind of the individual is left free to weigh important and difficult matters . . . There is no reason to believe in any such benign dispensation. The contrary is more likely to prevail. The individual tends to leave the important decisions to his institution while busying himself with [minor] tactics and details . . .

Mary Douglas,
How Institutions Think,
Syracuse University Press,
Syracuse, New York, 1986

A variety of labels have been proposed to characterize the present age. Some have claimed that we are in the "post-industrial age." Others have argued that we have entered the "atomic age." Still others have proposed that we are in the "information age," the "space age" or the "global era." While all of these are valid, they miss, however, a deeper and less visible aspect of modern society. The present era cannot be defined only in terms of its modes of production, sources of energy, the existence of a specific set of technologies, or where economic activities are conducted. What most distinguishes our society is that we have become a "technological society."

The development and use of technology provides a common and constant element that characterizes our times. This is indicated in a number of ways: the commitment of corporations to technological progress, the extent to which technological innovations for strategic advantage are constantly stressed. The government's overall commitment to new technological developments and R&D programs and its insistence that most current societal problems can be largely overcome through technological solutions are another indication. The very obviousness of these statements and the fact that they are taken for granted are themselves an indication of the importance of technology. Technology itself has become the new order, the fundamental nature of present society.

Perhaps because it is so self-evident, this very characteristic of society is often not acknowledged. The very fact that we are so dependent on technology has itself become "invisible." It is "taken for granted." To a certain extent, this very "invisibility" echoes the very nature of technology itself. Indeed, the whole point of many technologies is their "disappearing act." They must be taken for granted; especially in the case of dangerous technologies which must become "invisible" in order to be used without fear.

In 1934, Lewis Mumford[1] stressed the invisibility of technology. He noticed that after a short period of exuberance following the introduction of a new technology, it had the tendency to disappear and hence to be taken for granted in the society in which it was used. Mumford pointed out that during his time the printing press, watch, radio, telephone, telegraph, automobile, train, and even electricity itself all disappeared into the background of society. Today, we would add television, computers, computer software, video technologies, credit cards, cellular telephones, copy machines, satellite communications, fax machines, radar, digital recording, painkillers, X-rays, open heart surgery, robotics, and so on. It seems likely that in the near future, technologies such as lasers, "space technologies," and biogenetics will also be taken for granted. To use a marketing term, technologies tend to become "generic products." They are expected to be available and reliable, and in so doing, they become "quasi-invisible" in their day-to-day use.

1. L. Mumford, *Technics and Civilization.* New York: Harcourt, Brace and Co., 1934.

THE DANGERS ASSOCIATED WITH
THE INVISIBILITY OF TECHNOLOGIES

If invisibility is a sign that a given technology has been well accepted and integrated into society, and thus proven "successful," invisibility is also associated with two broad classes of danger. First, it allows a technology to be regarded as a "natural" characteristic, as if that technology had always existed and will always be available; as though it was provided by nature itself. Second, it is also associated with "technological habits." The users of a technology always become dependent on them, thus confusing means with ends. As a result, they are no longer able to know and to challenge the basic assumptions on which they are based.

In this chapter, we will discuss two such dangers and show how invisibility can threaten the survival of even large and powerful organizations. We also will show how these dangers can be avoided.

At the outset, it should be stressed that we are not "anti-technology," advocating that we return à la Rousseau to some "natural condition." Rather, we wish to challenge some of the basic assumptions that are made about technology and by so doing help organizations become less dependent on their most dangerous aspects.

As a result of our many interviews, it has become increasingly clear that the invisibility of technology is one of the most important causes of disasters and crises. Specifically, invisibility does not allow executives to fully understand how their companies are dependent on their very technologies for their day-to-day operations. As a result, they are not able to evaluate objectively the potential dangers associated with them. Crisis-Prepared as opposed to Crisis-Prone organizations understand the dangers associated with invisibility. They thus have implemented a set of highly specific actions for reducing these dangers.

TECHNOLOGIES DO NOT COME FROM GOD

The first danger of invisibility is the belief that a technology is "natural," that it has emerged from nature itself and is, in fact, part of nature. Once this is believed, a technology is then assumed to be as constant, available, and unlimited as natural resources themselves. The important point is that the belief in the "naturalness" of a technology and in its constant availability prevents its users from developing a set of contingency plans in case of its sudden disappearance.

One of the most striking examples of the negative effects of such beliefs is provided by the "Hinsdale crisis" that we referred to earlier. To briefly review its details, the Hinsdale disaster was triggered by a telecommunications outage in the Chicago area in 1988 which was itself triggered by a fire in one of the telecommunications network centers operated by Illinois Bell. Because of the importance of this connecting point in the total telephone network, more than 500,000 subscribers were left without phone communications during a period ranging from one day to three weeks. Considering the dependence of businesses upon the telephone for voice as well as for data communications, a conservative estimate of the cost of the Hinsdale crisis in terms of business losses and repairs has been evaluated at $300 million. However, at the time of this writing, a number of companies are suing Illinois Bell. Thus, the total cost could be much higher.

Given the importance of Hinsdale, we interviewed a total of thirty managers and executives who were affected by this particular outage. The overall conclusion can be summarized in a single sentence: *Most of those we interviewed rediscovered the importance of the telephone.* Most of the respondents in fact reported understanding this basic insight, however trivial it appears. Given the basic assumptions that managers held about the availability of the telephone technology, it is anything but trivial. One manager summarized it best when he said rather humorously: "We all know where the dial tone comes from . . . it comes from God!"

If Hinsdale has only one lesson to teach us, it is this: Companies that held tenaciously to the assumption of the "naturalness" of the telephone were ill-prepared for the crisis, and as a result, became dangerously Crisis Prone. Indeed, those companies that were identified as Crisis Prone were much more affected than companies that were Crisis Prepared—for instance, local hospitals, O'Hare Airport, local police, or fire and emergency services. When Crisis-Prone organizations had any plans at all for protecting their telecommunication systems, they focused on the three most commonly perceived and accepted levels of protection: 1) backing-up records and protecting access to computers; 2) protecting the buildings and the rooms in which their computers were located; and 3) protecting their own computer network. However, they did not consider the *total context* in which their telecommunications systems operated, the telephone network as a whole.

As four respondents put it: "We had redundancy before the outage
. . . but our thinking at that time was that the problem would be in *our*
system, not in the carrier network itself"; "The plans we made before
Hinsdale were directed with regard to our system, not the network";
"The contingency plans we made before Hinsdale were mostly focused internally"; or, "We took the telephone for granted; we backed-
up our own system and our own network but not the telephone system
or network itself."

While Hinsdale was a crisis triggered by a technological breakdown, it also generated a number of insights that have implications for
management in general extending far beyond technology itself. For
example, the sudden unavailability of the telephone caused respondents to reevaluate their assumptions with regard to the strict separation between voice and data communications. A number of executives
realized that their exclusive focus on the protection of accounting,
financial, or inventory data and their separation of voice and data communication in two different departments were inadequate. While acknowledging the paramount necessity of protecting the technical data,
they also stressed in addition the necessity of protecting voice communications, i.e, the "human side" of communication, the communication between people instead of between machines. As they put it:
"Our plans prior to the crisis focused exclusively on data, not voice
communication"; "We had no plans on the voice side; it was a matter
of policy to have contingency plans on the data side"; or "How could
our customers call us? This was very detrimental to our image."

A second danger associated with the belief in the "naturalness" of
technology is the growing incapacity to learn from crises, in many
cases the difficulty in considering the very possibility of a serious crisis. While most of the respondents rediscovered their dependency
upon the telephone, this insight has not spread to the general business
community at large. In fact, several respondents we interviewed did
not attribute the Hinsdale crisis to their previous belief in the "external
availability of the telephone." Rather, they blamed and "explained it
away" solely on mistakes due to Illinois Bell.

This insistence in "explaining crises away," focusing on a narrow
set of causes that seem to "justify" the crisis, making it "exceptional"
or "abnormal" or caused by "human error," is endemic to the belief in
the "naturalness of technology." We call this "denial by exception." It
allows us to reinforce the basic assumption that a particular technology

has emerged from nature itself and that its use is thereby obligatory, "natural," a "fact of life," a "given." In addition, and with very few exceptions, a crisis is then perceived as that which is caused by human errors, and not by nature.

In virtually every industry we have studied there is a strong tendency to "explain crises away" by the use of such mechanisms. Unfortunately, this neither prevents the particular crisis at hand nor does it prevent one from challenging other basic assumptions. For example, some have attempted to "explain away" the Bhopal disaster as an act of sabotage. This prevents us from challenging basic assumptions such as the "naturalness" of producing dangerous chemical products in a plant surrounded by a densely populated slum. The Exxon Valdez disaster has been "explained away" through the alcohol problems of Valdez's captain. As a result, this hampers us in challenging assumptions such as the "naturalness" of operating massive oil tankers in ecologically fragile areas. The Chernobyl nuclear disaster has been "explained away" by the specific technology used in the USSR without challenging basic assumptions such as the "naturalness" of operating giant nuclear facilities in populated areas.

A variation of the previous mechanism is what we call "denial by normalization." Through its use, the basic assumption of the "naturalness" of a given technology is unchallenged by normalizing and downplaying its negative effects. For example, the Challenger disaster was "normalized" through the claim that every new exploration has associated dangers, risks, and accidents. Also, the estimated 10,000 deaths a year associated with the production of power generated through coal, or the 50,000 persons killed a year on highways in the U.S. alone are taken as "facts of life," as "givens," as secondary and necessary effects of such technologies. Similarly, airline crashes are "normalized" by comparing them proportionally to car accidents. We will return later to the dangers of not questioning the basic assumption of the "naturalness" of technologies as if they were somehow "organically given." Suffice it to say that such assumptions hinder improvements or changes in systems and increase thereby the potential for accidents and disasters.

Finally, it should be noted that to achieve a state of "naturalness" or "invisibility" for a given technology is one of the most important goals for its developers. Indeed, the more that a dangerous technology can be made "invisible" to its users and the public at large, the more that it can be integrated into society, and consequently, the more it can generate financial rewards. This was expressed well by a public relations director we interviewed from a large gas company: "My job is to make our product invisible." However, if invisibility is one of the paramount conditions for a technology to be widely used in society, invisibility also has the tendency to increase the relative ignorance of its dangers by the very executives who manage it. An information systems manager in a large catalog sales company declared: "Our top executives do not fully understand our technology . . . they expect that it will simply 'work.'" Or in a large airline company: "We do not have executive support for enhancing our technology; in many areas we are walking right on the edge of a major disaster."

The danger of believing in the naturalness of technology can be summarized as follows: While as a society we have learned often painfully about the dangerous aspects of technologies that are used for long periods of time (such as asbestos), we are not yet fully aware of the dangerous aspects or consequences of the technologies we have adopted or developed more recently. As a result, few contingency plans have been developed. This is tantamount to inviting crises to happen. For this reason, it is important to stress once again, those companies that had understood prior to the Hinsdale crisis that "the dial tone does *not* come from God" were minimally affected by the crisis.

THE DANGERS ASSOCIATED WITH "TECHNOLOGICAL HABITS"

The second major danger of the invisibility of technology is the formation of "technological habits." The mechanisms we have already discussed, i.e., the invisibility of technologies, belief in their naturalness, or "denial by exception" and "denial by normalization," maintain and reinforce a habit of using technologies as a panacea for solving problems. By saying this, we do not mean that habit formation is thereby to be avoided at all costs. Habits are indeed one of the powerful mechanisms by which a society maintains itself.

If habits are necessary, they can also become dangerous when actions that occur as their result turn around to reinforce them. In this case, what was previously a healthy habit turns into a dangerous addiction. St. Thomas observed wisely that a "mortal sin" was a sin that when it was committed encouraged others to commit it as well. Today, the modern sciences of cybernetics and systems theory call such destructive self-developing forces "deviation-amplifying loops" or "vicious circles." In such cases, a behavior or a habit grows without bounds, leading to chaos and disaster in the absence of any corrective forces.

During our interviews, we encountered numerous instances where the use of advanced technologies led to dangerous vicious circles. In such cases, the use of advanced and complex technologies led to the use of still more advanced and complex technologies, each turn of the vicious circle making organizations ever more dependent upon them. For example, during the Hinsdale crisis, travel agencies that lost use of their computers had to shut down their operations because their reservation, routing, and pricing processes were too complex to be otherwise performed. Similarly, large insurance companies ceased operations, the complexity of processing claims having become too complicated to be performed without the use of computers. Countless other examples such as accounting processes, payroll, inventories, catalog sales, robotics, etc., could be named as well. In each case, it is not clear if the availability of the technology itself has created the resultant complexity in procedures, or if the need for more complex procedures has pushed technology to accommodate itself to complexity. To some extent, the answer is trivial. What is important to notice is that through the existence of vicious circles, complexity has increased both the procedures and the technologies themselves, the ultimate danger being near-total dependence on them. We should also note that increased complexity and further dependency are themselves largely invisible. In fact, new technologies are constantly introduced for managing increased complexity and are viewed by their users as the logical solution to their ongoing problems. Often, only a crisis can break through such circles by suddenly making the invisibility of an organization's "technological habits" visible again.

Perhaps the single best example of the dangers associated with the invisibility of technologies and "technological habits" can be found in information systems. While information technologies were first presented as the solution for managing complex information problems more efficiently, thus giving organizations increased freedom and productivity, one of the downsides of such improvements is that organizations have become extremely dependent on them. Present estimates in the U.S. are that some 85 percent of corporations are now heavily or totally dependent on information technology. According to a recent study, it is estimated that all companies across all industries will lose on average 25 percent of their daily revenues after the sixth day of an information system breakdown.[2] This figure is close to 40 percent for the financial and banking industries and for public utilities. The point is not that modern industry needs to return to manual processes. This is as absurd as it is impossible. Rather, the point is that all executives need to become more aware of the current dangerous dependency of their corporations on such technologies. As stressed by a manager in a large insurance company, "To throw hardware and money on problems is a dangerous strategy." It reinforces the—mostly invisible—vicious circle of "technological habits."

The current dependency of corporations on advanced technologies would not be so important an issue were it not for the fact that advanced technological systems have two additional characteristics: They are often very fragile and, further, their fragility is itself mostly invisible until a crisis happens.

The fragility of advanced technical systems has been well demonstrated by Charles Perrow.[3] In his path-breaking analysis, Perrow points to two inherent characteristics of advanced technologies, "complexity" and "tight-coupling," that render technological systems dangerously Crisis Prone. "Complexity" refers to the number of components and the number of relationships existing between them in a given technological and social system. "Tight-coupling" refers to the degree of slack or buffer between each component, a variation in one triggering variation in another. These two characteristics were instrumental to the 1987 stock market crash. The complexity of the world's information system network and its tight-coupling, i.e., a change in New York triggering a change in Tokyo, contributed to the magnitude of the crisis. Notice that prior to the crisis both the complexity and the tight-coupling of the system were mostly "invisible," and thus, not commonly thought of as a potential threat.

The fragility of advanced technological systems is due basically to the fact that there is a coupling between complexity and tight-coupling itself. These two characteristics make systems extremely sensitive to even minor changes. In the fields of atmospheric research and chaos

2. Paul Tate, "Risk! The Third Factor," *Datamation*, April 18, 1988.
3. C. Perrow, *Normal Accidents. Living With High-Risk Technologies*. New York: Basic Books, 1984.

theory,[4] this fragility is referred to as the "butterfly effect." The metaphor refers to the "fact" that the flap of the butterfly's wing in one part of the world can trigger a large atmospheric change, such as a cyclone, in another. "Butterfly effects" are common in industrial crises. The Chernobyl catastrophe was triggered by a standard security procedure; the Challenger disaster was triggered by a break in a simple mechanical part; the 1984 Tokyo telecommunication outage was triggered by a regular maintenance effort; a plant of the Virginia Electric Power company was shut down for four days in 1980 after an employee's shirt pocket caught on a handle of a circuit breaker; the Hinsdale crisis was triggered by the accidental connection of two ordinary wires. The point of these examples is that the invisible fragility of advanced technological systems springs from the invisibility of triggering events themselves.

Many of the triggering events of major crises are trivial and insignificant. They are often as trivial as the "flap of a butterfly's wing." Of course, we are not arguing that minor incidents in themselves "cause" major crises. Rather, we are saying that small variations can "trigger" crises if they are amplified through tight relationships with other elements in a complex system. For example, the triggering event of the Bhopal disaster—the mixing of a highly toxic material with water—would not have developed into a major crisis if it had not been amplified by a great number of other factors that were both technical and human. A simplified list of these other factors includes the presence of small impurities in the concerned tank triggering unanticipated chemical transformations; the unavailability of diverse safety features; the chemical complexity of the gas released which did not allow scientists to diagnose it with certainty to determine proper health treatment; the proximity of thousands of people to the plant; multiple human errors; the ignorance by the local population and emergency personnel about the potential dangers; the lack of expertise on the part of the plant's top management; the lowering of morale of the plant's employees and managers triggered by Union Carbide's previous decision to divest itself of the facility; and many more.[5]

Numerous industrial crises have taught us that it is impossible to point to merely one or two major "causes" of a disaster. In some sense, the causes themselves are also "invisible," considering their

4. James Gleick, *Chaos, Making a New Science*. New York: Viking, 1987.
5. For an in-depth analysis of Bhopal, see Shrivastava, *op. cit.*

relative insignificance, the large number of factors involved, and the complexity of their interactions. Thus, it is impossible to point to one or two major "causes" of the Challenger, Chernobyl, or Valdez disasters. To attempt to do so is to rely on the mechanism of "denial by exception." The very use of this mechanism leads us to deny threats posed by the *total system of interactions* between technology and people, and to reinforce the global invisibility of technologies and their potential dangers, a truly dangerous vicious circle.

Consider again the example of Hinsdale. To blame the crisis only on deficiencies existing within the Illinois Bell system is to invite similar crises to happen in the future. As stated in the study conducted by the state fire marshal after the crisis, a Hinsdale-type crisis could potentially occur across the entire nation. At present, more than 11,500 centers such as at Hinsdale exist in the U.S. telephone network in addition to 9,000 more minor transmission stations. This is not to say that all such facilities are subject to the same degree of risk as Hinsdale. However, to blame the crisis only on the inefficiency of the operating telephone company hinders the possibility of conducting a risk assessment of each situation. Indeed, similar crises happened in Tokyo in 1984 and in Brooklyn, New York, in 1987, both crises resulting in business losses in the hundreds of millions. Further, to assume that Hinsdale is an "exception" is to increase a company's vulnerability to terrorism and sabotage. A number of executives we interviewed stated, "We learned that a terrorist, or a disgruntled employee, could wipe out the entire system." Stated even more bluntly: "Hinsdale is a blueprint for terrorism."

If all technologies thus have the tendency to "disappear into the woodwork" after a while, they also have the tendency to reappear in the form of disasters and crises. In other words, vicious circles have a built-in, natural corrective feature, the breakdown of the entire system! A worrisome example is the present proliferation of viruses in computer software. At present, it is evaluated that 40 percent of the largest U.S. firms have been affected. Considering that the problem involves both tremendous complexity and tight-coupling between technological systems and human behavior, most of those we interviewed declared that their actions were relatively limited for responding to the threat. As stated by one manager in a large oil company: "We cannot act on individual workstations. They are too independent. We can only protect our mainframe system"; or, as one executive in an insurance company put it: "So far, we have limited ourselves to restricting access to our mainframe; we do not 'advertise' viruses. We do not wish to give 'bad ideas' to our employees."

Crisis-Prepared organizations on the other hand understand much more fully that all technologies have the dangerous tendency to disappear first and then to become visible again through crises. In the following section, we indicate how some of them have attempted to make the invisibility of technologies visible again prior to a crisis.

"MANAGEMENT BY NOSING AROUND": EXPOSING THE INVISIBILITY OF TECHNOLOGIES

While the principle of "Management by Walking Around" has been advocated by Peters and Waterman,[6] we have found that "Management by Nosing Around" is the principle that Crisis-Prepared organizations use for understanding better the interactions between people and complex technologies. Central to this is making visible the invisibility of technologies and probing deeply into their potential dangers. Through our 350 interviews, we have discovered a number of very creative processes that have been implemented with success.

1) *Challenging "technological habits"*: Crisis-Prepared organizations understand the necessity for systematically challenging their "technological habits." They attempt to develop a "multiple outlook culture" by hiring a number of people with different backgrounds and expertise. For example, one chemical company has invited two representatives of an ecological group to serve on its board of directors; another company in the oil industry has hired staff with no experience in the industry and with no background in technology at all in order to challenge taken-for-granted beliefs and assumptions; other companies have hired consultants with the explicit and prime purpose that they become "insultants," to use Peter Drucker's apt phrase, in an attempt to challenge basic assumptions as well.

2) *Diminishing technological complexity*: Crisis-Prepared organizations have also undertaken the task of understanding the vicious circles that are involved in attempting to resolve ever more complex problems with ever more complex technologies. Whenever possible, they attempt to reduce the overall complexity of their entire opera-

6. *Op. cit.*

tions. For example, in one oil company, top management made the decision to freeze as much as possible the acquisition of new technologies if the task could be done with existing ones; in an insurance company, an attempt was made to de-automate the processing of claims.

3) *Budgeting "dependency costs"*: Closely related to the previous strategy, other Crisis-Prepared organizations go beyond traditional cost-benefit analyses for evaluating the acquisition of new technologies. They have added to their standard evaluations a "dependency cost," i.e., an evaluation of the cost to the organization if their technologies failed. Thus, such organizations do not only evaluate their potential costs for maintenance, repair, or emergencies. They also evaluate—and this is the fundamental point—the costs due to lost business if their technologies suddenly collapsed. This is to say that these organizations have formally made visible costs that were largely invisible. Recently, a large insurance company refused to purchase a multimillion dollar information system on precisely this basis. They reached the conclusion that too great a dependency on a particular technology constituted a competitive *dis*advantage.

4) *Scanning for "prodomes"*: Most Crisis-Prepared organizations scan for "prodomes," i.e., advance, early warning signals of crises and near-crises that have happened in the past. They understand that most crises have prodomes and have a dynamic that can be studied by appropriate processes. For example, a total of thirty-seven crises *larger* than the Exxon Valdez disaster took place prior to Valdez, but outside U.S. waters; crises similar to Hinsdale happened previously in New York City, Tokyo, and Brooklyn; or the Challenger disaster was preceded by a trail of memos that warned explicitly of the danger. To scan for prodomes is to go beyond "denial by exception." It is to take the occurrence of crises seriously. Some large organizations have already included scanning in their existing Issues Management Programs; others have hired specialized staff to track specific issues.

5) *Probing for tampering*: Crisis-Prepared organizations have also gone far beyond traditional strategic analyses of their vulnerabilities which focus on competitive moves, market fluctuations, regulatory changes, etc. In addition to these, they also challenge various invisibilities associated with their products and processes. For example, one large pharmaceutical company has explicitly created an "internal assassin team" which attempts explicitly to tamper with the company's products and production processes. It also has created a "counter-

assassin team" which attempts to protect its products and processes from the assassin team. As a result, this company has introduced a number of products and production changes that are more resistant to tampering and terrorism.

6) *Introducing "buffering mechanisms"*: Drawing from what they have learned about "prodomes" and their enhanced vulnerability analyses, some organizations have introduced a number of buffering mechanisms for protecting their most important tasks. To do this, they first prioritized their operations, distinguishing carefully between tasks which were considered most urgent and paramount and those which were less so. Next, they introduced a number of "buffer mechanisms" for protecting their most critical tasks or operations. These buffers include the creation of a "crisis management unit"; technical changes such as a rerouting of information system networks or redundancies that are added to their most crucial technologies; contingency plans for a redeployment of personnel; alternative strategies for the production or distribution of products and services; etc. However, and this is the important point, while Crisis-Prone organizations attempt to buffer potential threats by *adding* to the complexity of their technological systems, Crisis-Prepared organizations attempt to diminish the extent of their tight-coupling *without substantially adding* to the overall complexity of their operations.

7) *Rewarding reliability*: Most Crisis-Prepared organizations also reward reliability. Some organizations have explicitly introduced different bonus packages to reward those employees responsible for ensuring trouble-free operations. Others systematically reward "whistleblowers," thus increasing the organization's ability to profit from the elimination of potential threats and dangers that were previously invisible. It soon becomes very clear from even the briefest stay in such organizations that they have developed an internal culture where discussions of "bad news" are not only tolerated but even encouraged. Indeed, employees are rewarded formally for pointing out problems. Above all, the attitude "If it ain't broke, don't fix it" is *not* tolerated; indeed, such expressions almost become grounds for immediate dismissal. If anything, a counter-principle operates: "If it ain't broke, then probe it for potential breaks before it becomes too big to fix!"

8) *Commemorating crises*: Instead of attempting to forget past crises as soon as possible and making them taboo subjects for discussion, Crisis-Prepared organizations also systematically celebrate the

anniversaries of their most important crises, emphasizing both their mistakes and successes. Such organizations understand fundamentally that to acknowledge unfortunate events formally is much more healthy and productive than denying them. They also understand the necessity of sustaining the visibility of the dangers of their technologies. Further, they are conscious that even in the absence of formal acknowledgment, managers and employees alike painfully remember such crises anyway. It is not a secret and it is understandable that some executives at Johnson & Johnson, for instance, have nightmares on the anniversary dates of the Tylenol tragedies. Above all, the occasions are used as opportunities for learning with regard to what can be done even better. They are *not* used as occasions for finding scapegoats and for blaming.

Managers in one large food organization wear black armbands to symbolize mourning on the anniversary of their most important crises; other companies have institutionalized mourning ceremonies as symbols of such events. The government of Mexico has implemented a policy of displaying wrecked cars along freeways in order to symbolize the dangers inherent in surpassing the speed limit.

9) *Rigorously studying past crises*: Crisis-Prepared organizations also understand the necessity of systematically studying past crises and implementing changes based on learning. For example, one food company has merged its data management department with its voice telecommunication unit after its experience of Hinsdale; another has formally decided to stop "throwing hardware and money on problems." Other companies realistically simulate crises by hiring improvisational actors to portray media representatives, customers, government officials or terrorists. The assumption is that trained actors can "get into the roles much better and much more realistically" than professionals. What seems characteristic of all Crisis-Prepared organizations is their deep understanding that proper crisis management extends far beyond written manuals. They believe in personal training, direct experience, and actual simulations.

10) *Championing the challenging of basic assumptions*: Lastly, all Crisis-Prepared organizations exhibit a similar commitment by their CEOs and top executives to challenging their basic assumptions about technology. The top management of such organizations recognize the tremendous financial and human costs involved if a company remains Crisis Prone. They also believe that to become Crisis Prepared is a

paramount—but still largely ignored—competitive advantage. Ironically, these organizations are often the ones that have directly experienced some of the most important industrial crises in the past. However, as opposed to Crisis-Prone organizations, they have allowed themselves to learn from their own worst experiences.

To develop a Crisis-Prepared culture is, to say the least, difficult. Invisible "technological habits" do not merely influence technologies alone. In a "technological society," to use De Tocqueville's nice way of wording it, they also become the "habits of the heart" of the general culture itself. In this sense, the two characteristics of advanced technologies, complexity and tight-coupling, strongly influence the way corporations are managed on a day-to-day basis: Complexity leads to the belief that "bigger is better," or that "greater complexity is better than simplicity." They also lead to further beliefs such as "faster is also better." Notice that these very themes are often those that are advocated most in order that corporations can increase their competitive edge and survive in the new global marketplace. To a "certain extent," such beliefs are indeed correct. Innovation and responsiveness *do* require speed and power. However, as we have seen, these two characteristics are also the very ones that increase the dependency of corporations on advanced technologies as well as increase the total fragility of technological systems themselves.

The fact that such "habits of the heart" are still largely invisible and unconscious has consequences which are paradoxical. Attempts at achieving even greater competitiveness and flexibility can in some cases lead to more dependency and fragility. In the medical field, this effect is called "iatrogenic." It is expressed in the notion "The operation was successful, but the patient is dead." *An iatrogenic solution is thus a "successful solution" that worsens the problem.* To attempt even to expose the invisibility of a technology is in fact to address some of the iatrogenic effects of technologies, a most difficult task in a society which is as strongly technological as ours! And yet, if we are to avoid future disasters, this is precisely what we must attempt to do.

Part III

SOCIETAL GAMES

Chapter 8

Mass Media: The Unreality Game

Nonfiction TV has become more diversified and more democratic. Sure, in this vast array there are differences in quality. Yes, from time to time there are excesses. For example, there is too much reliance on so-called dramatizations, and maybe I could have found a more sanitary way to define ritual devil worship. But who can deny that, overall, news programming is now more interesting, vital and less pretentious?

Face it, the old-style network news documentaries have become boring. Yes, they were critical darlings, but the television audience got tired of being lectured down to by reporters sitting up on a journalistic Mount Olympus. Even the networks have adjusted. "West 57th Street" is a long way from "CBS Reports."

At some point, even the ivory tower elite will recognize that an audience numbering in the tens of millions is not a lunatic fringe nor a gullible cult. It is America, and it is watching.

Geraldo Rivera, "TV's Wave
of the Future," *The New York Times*,
December 6, 1988, p. A 19

It is a staggering news story—the crumbling of communism as the sole official truth in the nations of eastern Europe and now even in the Soviet Union. There will not be many bigger stories this century, if ever. Yet the TV networks, try as they may,

simply seem unable to get a grasp on the monumental proportions of the almost surreal events. There is a reason:

Television news is finally paying the price for what it has let
itself become—increasingly shallow and trivial, with endless and
meaningless tidbits on show biz, airhead local anchors, inane
sports reporters, clownish weathermen, all combining to create
an audience that is turned off by lengthy discussion and depth.
Except when the *real* in-depth reporters—Oprah and Geraldo
and Donahue and Sally Jessee—deal with the genuinely important stuff.

Viewers are getting wise to them. But it may be too late,
because viewers may now be the real problem—brainwashed
into acceptance of triviality and unable any longer to sit still for a
talking-heads discussion or for the good, solid documentaries
and instant prime-time news reports that used to be on every
week.

Something has really got to happen to prevent viewers from
getting dumber and shallower about current events because of
TV news. You have to wonder how much the increasing lack of
depth and perspective in TV news is contributing to the dreadful
history scores in surveys of high school subjects.

Will the lessening of substance in TV news allow events to
fall more and more into the formats of revisionist docudramas
that make up facts, tabloid shows that don't care about them and
sensationalist talk-show hosts who unblinkingly allow celebrity
guests to fill the air with fibs and fluff?

In the end, though, it's not TV news we have to worry about.
It's us.

Stay tuned. Or better yet, don't.

Rick Dubrow, "TV News Too Trivial to See
the Big Picture," Los Angeles Times,
February 10, 1990, pp. F1 & F6

We come at last to the games that are played at the level of U.S.
society as a whole.

Given the incredible hold that the Fragmentation game exerts on
the general psyche of Western societies—the extreme compartmentali-
zation of reality into disconnected and seemingly unrelated parts by

means of abstract concepts and distinctions that more and more are arbitrary—we're going to make what appears to be an extreme jump. We're going to turn to a phenomenon that on its surface seems totally unrelated to what we have previously been discussing. And yet, the more two phenomena seem superficially unrelated, the more that beneath the surface they are related.

If one of the major effects of the games we have discussed previously is the potential for larger and larger threats to the physical environment, then the major effect of the games described in this chapter is the threat they pose to our mental and conceptual environment. In this sense, this chapter deals with a major crisis as well, although of a somewhat different kind. However, in today's world the line between the two kinds is increasingly thin. Because of the enormous impact of the electronic media in modern societies, they have literally altered the very ways in which we think, conceptualize, and even experience reality. The electronic media impact seriously on how we both report and react to major crises. As such, they have the potential to impact not only what we experience as crises, and how, but even more fundamentally, what we even define as crises. The "bottom line" of our discussion is that technology poses a major threat not only to our physical well-being on a scale never before realized in human history, but to our mental well-being as well. However, since the threats posed by the electronic media are in general even more invisible than those we have discussed previously, we should expect that the denial of their effects will be even stronger. And indeed, this is precisely what we shall find.

There is no need for us to repeat in its entirety the list of games we have encountered previously, for the same basic set are played at this level of reality or human affairs as well. In addition, we're not going to discuss a whole host of other games which are exceedingly important in their own right—such as the Disinformation game that, unfortunately, is widely played by both government and private institutions alike; the Greed and Wealth Accumulation game that assumed such prominence especially during the Reagan years; the Blame the Poor game; Pick on Women and Other Minorities game, etc. While all these are important, they are not our main concern. Instead, we're going to focus on one major game and show how our major energies as a society increasingly have been channeled into its playing. We are also going to show how most of the games we have encountered previously serve as subgames to this major game. The games we have identified previously are not only activated by this larger game, of which the subgames are merely parts, but their activation serves to maintain the larger one as well.

In a recent book entitled *The Unreality Industry*,[1] Mitroff and Warren Bennis described a phenomenon that especially since the 1960s has come to dominate much of American life. Although it was not labeled as such in this prior book, it can be called the Unreality game. The Unreality game is by now so dominant and so pervasive a force in American life, if not increasingly around the world, that it influences nearly everything that Americans do. Casting the phenomenon of unreality into a game which is both activated and maintained by the subgames we have identified previously allows us to bring out additional important elements of unreality that Mitroff and Bennis were not able to elucidate, let alone treat effectively, in their earlier book.

Because the Unreality game is a direct reflection as well as an outgrowth of the American experience, it cannot therefore either be appreciated or understood without some broader understanding of the general values and forces that have shaped U.S. society. Since neither the province of U.S. history nor a full account of it are our primary concerns, we must of necessity adopt a shortcut approach in describing what it is in the broader American experience that has made U.S. society so especially vulnerable to unreality. While a shortcut approach must inevitably leave out many important details and qualifications, it has the decisive advantage of clearly focusing our attention on the crucial elements of the phenomenon at hand.

One of the most powerful ways, perhaps *the most* powerful, to get to the root of the crucial experiences that have shaped any society is to examine its central myths—the decisive, critical stories that it tells itself over and over again in order to reassure as well as reaffirm itself. As we have seen previously, when the assumptions that constitute the belief system or systems of both individuals and organizations are shattered, by whatever means, then truly an existential dilemma or crisis of major proportions may be said to exist. At such times, individuals and organizations not only search desperately for but grasp whatever devices are available to prop them up. The preoccupation with unreality that seems to dominate so much of current life in U.S.

1. Ian I. Mitroff and Warren Bennis, *The Unreality Industry: The Deliberate Manufacturing of Falsehood and What It Is Doing to Our Lives*. New York: Birch Lane Press, 1989.

society is almost a direct response to the fact that many of our most sacred and cherished values either no longer exist, certainly not in their original intended forms, or have been so debased as to be a parody of their earlier selves. In a word, the game of Unreality exists to comfort and to shield us from the fact that we are only the vaguest representation of the values for which we once stood. Unreality exists primarily to keep us from facing directly what secretly all of us know, that the U.S. has lost much of its earlier spiritual and physical preeminence. We are, in short, a hollow resemblance of what we once were. Great powers rise and fall not merely, as Yale historian Paul Kennedy[2] has written about so persuasively, because their structural and physical entanglements have greatly overstepped their resources, but because in addition, their basic beliefs have become a hollow vestige of what they once were [see Box 1 in the appendices].

Fortunately, the task of examining the major myths/stories/values of U.S. society has been rendered almost trivial due to the efforts of two eminent scholars, Robert Reich[3] and Rupert Wilkinson.[4] Each, in his own way, and without any apparent knowledge of the other, has described four major myths or themes that purport to capture the major myths/stories/values of U.S. society. For Wilkinson, the primary values and driving forces behind U.S. society are captured in four major fears:

(1) the Fear of Being Owned
(2) the Fear of Falling Apart
(3) the Fear of Falling Away
(4) the Fear of Winding Down.

For Reich, they are represented in four major myths or stories:

(1) the Mob at the Gates
(2) the Rot at the Top
(3) the Triumphant Individual
(4) the Benevolent Society.

For Reich and Wilkinson alike, each of their four respective fac-

---

2. Paul Kennedy, *The Rise and Fall of Great Powers: Economic Change and Military Conflict From 1500 to 2000.* New York: Random House, 1987.
3. Robert Reich, *Tales of a New America.* New York: Times Books, 1987.
4. Rupert Wilkinson, *The Pursuit of American Character.* New York: Harper and Row, 1988.

tors are so fundamental that over the entire course of U.S. history, Americans have (1) explained their condition, (2) defined and recognized their important problems, (3) sought solutions to them, and (4) framed important initiatives and programs in terms of them. While the particulars of the stories have varied dramatically over the course of our history, the basic themes themselves have not.

The Fear of Being Owned is one of the earliest and perhaps most basic and primitive of all the fears that Americans share. It derives rather obviously from the major factor which caused our forefathers to leave Europe and emigrate to America: the long-suffered oppression at the hands of European kings and nobility. Because of the power and depth with which this particular fear is engrained in the American experience, if not psyche, it has instilled a deep distrust of centralized big government and all large institutions in general. As such, it figures predominantly in the current debate regarding whether the U.S. needs an Industrial Policy, i.e., a coherent and deliberately orchestrated policy at the national level in order to give support for promising industries. To carry out such a policy means of course concentrating and centralizing in some government agency the necessary intelligence, power, and resources to carry out effectively such an important and momentous task.

Because the Fear of Being Owned remains largely unconscious in the American psyche, it is difficult to address the merits versus the demerits of an industrial policy on rational grounds alone. The U.S. is now competing in a world economy against other players such as Japan, South Korea, and West Germany, players who have successful industrial policies because they believe that government must be a firm ally and not a feared adversary. This is still a very difficult and foreign concept for Americans to accept. On the surface we can understand rationally that, in order to compete effectively, labor and management as well as U.S. industry and government must forge close ties and overcome past adversarial relationships and mutual fears. However, underneath it all, the Fear of Being Owned is still every bit alive and well. Precisely because so much of it remains unconscious, the fear is even more difficult to attack head-on.

The Fear of Falling Apart is captured, if not represented, by all the mutual antagonisms, conflicts, and strains that exist in a society as big, complex, divisive, and varied as ours. The Fear of Falling Apart is that we will be overwhelmed and literally destroyed by all the problems of a complex society: crime, racial unrest, alcoholism, drugs, the terrible fate of the homeless, the up and down roller coaster state of the economy, our huge trade deficits, etc. The fear is that our problems have become so big, so monumental, so impossible for anyone to state cogently, let alone treat effectively, that they will literally kill the American experiment. At the level of the individual, it is seen in our constant obsession with fads, the latest being the "health and exercise craze." At a personal level at least, the fear is symbolized by the desire to have a perfect face, body, family, home, life, personality, lest one disintegrate personally.

The Fear of Falling Away is the fear of abandoning the ideals of the American dream as laid down by the Founding Fathers. It is the fear of abandoning our spiritual heritage. In coming to America, our forefathers were not just journeying to a new geography or physical landscape. They were founding a new spiritual and moral landscape. This was the essence of their journey. America was to become and serve as a moral beacon to the world. The journey did not represent merely a beginning for the Pilgrims, but, rather, a beginning for all mankind. The uniqueness of the American experiment was to be that of starting a country literally from scratch untainted by the corruption of the Old World.

The Fear of Winding Down is the fear that we have lost the abiding and boundless energy of the people who founded and settled the land. Of all of the fears, this one in particular is perhaps most easily recognized in everyday life. America is bristling with so much energy that it screams from its pores as few other societies ever have. As our colleague Warren Bennis reminds us, "in America there is plenty of action and activity everywhere, but precious little channeling of it into purposeful direction or accomplishment."

Given the tremendous upheaval that was experienced by mind and body alike in the uprooting that was involved in leaving the Old World, the perilousness of the journey involved, the frightful conditions that were experienced during the first winters in the new land, plus the oppressive history from which we sprang, each of these fears or motifs makes perfect sense. This is perhaps even easier to appreciate if we examine from a psychoanalytic perspective the dynamics behind each of the fears. We will do this after we have examined Reich's four myths since the dynamics will be even easier to see then.

The Mob at the Gates is the fear that unless America is constantly on guard, it will be overrun by the barbarians just outside our walls who would rob us of our very riches, and even destroy us if only they could get in. Given the strong moral and religious fervor of the Founding Fathers as expressed in their abiding belief that they were establishing a nation that would serve as a moral example to all who had escaped terrible oppression, it is rather easy to see how the foundation for a strong psychological wall between an "us" and a "them" was being laid, perhaps for our entire history.

The Rot at the Top is the perennial myth that the common people themselves are the repository of all goodness and instinctive common wisdom. If America has been betrayed, then it is by the powerful at the top who, like European royalty, have become corrupted by unchecked power.

The Triumphant Individual is of course the quintessential American lone wolf, the solitary American hero who gets things done in his own quiet and determined way, who marches to his own drum unconcerned for what the masses or the mobs may think. He has assumed various cloaks and guises over our history. At one time he has been a Charles Lindbergh. At another, a John Wayne, and a Clint Eastwood in still another time period.

The Benevolent Society is of course America herself, the perennial champion of the underdog, the provider to the tired, the poor, the hungry, the downtrodden of the planet yearning to be set free. It is an America that can do no wrong because America herself is the fountainhead of all that is right.

In psychoanalytic terms, the Rot at the Top is of course the primal Oedipal fear, the dread that results from the bad father, the evil kings from which we fled originally. Given that conditions of serfdom and servitude thrust even supposed mature adults back into a state of childhood dependency, America's Oedipal fears have an all-too-real basis indeed. As we have learned, the human animal is inclined to exaggerate Oedipal fears even in the best of childhoods. The exaggeration then must become even more extreme and especially intense when there is some basis for it in fact. Thus, the Mob at the Gates is our unchecked projection of the evil originally done to us by kings onto all of America's enemies, real as well as imagined. Also, since no people are ever perfect, the Mob at the Gates is the unconscious projection of our own internal defects, our own acknowledged evil sides, onto others. The Benevolent Society is of course the good, nurturing, beneficent mother, while the Triumphant Individual is the young ego, unfettered by any past or sense of history, strutting forth brashly on the world stage.

While we shall not bother to make the connections more formally and systematically, it is easy to see that the Fear of Winding Down is the fear of losing the energy associated with the forever youthful Triumphant Individual. Similarly, the Fear of Falling Away is the companion fear of losing the virtues and graces associated with the Benevolent Society. The relationship between Wilkinson's remaining two fears and Reich's is a bit more complicated. The Fear of Being Owned is the fear of being overwhelmed or ruled by either the Mob at the Gates and/or the Rot at the Top. The Fear of Falling Apart is the fear of disintegrating, splitting or flying apart, literally dying from either the Mob at the Gates and/or the Rot at the Top.

With these notions in mind, we are ready to describe the game of unreality.

THE UNREALITY GAME

The fundamental purpose of the "Busy-ness" games we described earlier is to maintain the structure of those individuals whose "self" is weak or threatened. The same games were also involved in maintaining the weak or threatened self of Crisis-Prone organizations. In a similar fashion, *the primary purpose of the Unreality game is to maintain the myths of U.S. society*. The Unreality game does this by creating the illusion of a simpler world in which America is forever young, preeminently good, eminently fair, firmly in charge, and rooted out of all evil. To accomplish this, the game employs the tools of (a) nonstop, trivializing, and diverting entertainment; (b) the unparalleled production, glorification, worship, and consumption of celebrities on a scale not realized before in human history; (c) the endless production and infiltration of a dazzling array of electronic gadgets into our very consciousness;[5] (d) the unrelenting assault on our senses by an overwhelming volume of supposed "information" with which we are daily

---

5. We are not exaggerating. For instance, consider: "Michael McGreevy says that he will walk on the planet Venus within the next two years. But he plans to do it without leaving his laboratory in California's Silicon Valley. McGreevy, 40-year-old research scientist with . . . [NASA], is one of dozens of American and Japanese scientists racing to perfect a newly developed computer technology called virtual reality. The technology involves the use of computers to create full-color, three-dimensional images of everything from molecules to planetary surfaces. And rather than merely looking at the images, scientists are using headgear

bombarded (from the arcane and esoteric to the titillating and trivial, mixed in proportions that would tax even the most sophisticated alchemists); (e) the alteration of our physical landscape into a seemingly endless sea of carefully designed shopping malls whose primary purpose is to induce a state of intense anxiety that can be satisfied only by the instantaneous gratification that is derived from the purchase of goods. In other words, to maintain the myths of American society it is not only necessary to block out reality, but to create a whole set of interwoven "artificial realities" that perpetuate the myth that we are still in control.

As Mitroff and Bennis noted in their earlier book, *The Unreality Industry*, one of the clearest arenas in which to observe the operation of unreality in present day America is that of TV. This does *not* mean that TV is the only arena or culprit in which to observe the phenomenon of unreality or that TV is solely responsible for it. To repeat, TV is *merely one* of the best arenas in which to observe the phenomenon, not the only place where it occurs.

At the same time, it is not a random accident that TV has become the most powerful and dominant medium of American society. TV could not have attained this position unless it was a strong reflection of its preeminent values and interests.

America is the quintessential land of self-made people. Instead of being born into a society where one's station in life is determined or fixed by birth, everyone in America is "free," in theory at least, to rise as high or to fall as low as their native or developed talents will take them. Unlike more traditional societies where, relatively speaking, one has no need to be "known" or "famous" outside of a small, select circle—indeed being born into such a circle confirms its own fame—in American society being famous is a prerequisite to worldly success.[6] And since being successful is due not merely to one's native skills but dependent upon one's abilities to attract or draw attention to oneself, America is not only the quintessential land of self-made but of self-

---

resembling scuba diving masks with image-bearing screens to enter the so-called virtual realities and even manipulate their contents. There are also potentially tantalizing applications for the entertainment industry. Some theorists predict that people who now watch steamy TV sex videos could instead experience the sensation of participating in them." D'Arcy Jenish, "Recreating Reality, A New Development Has Tantalizing Applications," *Maclean's*, June 4, 1990, pp. 56-57.

6. Leo Braudy, *The Frenzy of Renown, Fame and Its History*. New York: Oxford University Press, 1986.

promoted people. Richard Schickel, the *Time* magazine film critic, has pointed out that in sharp contrast to earlier periods of human history, self-promotion has come to depend less and less upon actual achievement or accomplishment and more and more on the development and projection of one's image.[7] However superficial it may be, fame and success in contemporary American society depend more and more upon how one looks and sounds, what one appears to be, rather than on what one "really is." It is no wonder then why someone like Zsa Zsa Gabor would have become "famous for being famous," i.e., famous for merely being Zsa Zsa, and not for having accomplished anything substantial or worthwhile:

> Style, more and more, has become the official idiom of the marketplace. In advertising, packaging, product design, and corporate *identity* [emphasis in original], the power of provocative services speaks to the eye's mind, overshadowing matters of quality or substance. Style, moreover, is an intimate component of subjectivity, intertwined with people's aspirations and anxieties. Increasingly, style has emerged as a decisive component of politics; political issues and politicians are regularly subjected to the cosmetic sorcery of image managers, providing the public with a telegenic commodity. Democratic choice, like grocery shopping, has become a question of which product is most attractively packaged, which product is most imaginatively merchandised . . .[8]

TV is the perfect medium to exploit such tendencies in the American character. It exploits and feeds on our inherent narcissism, our central abiding belief that from our very inception we were destined to be the most moral nation on the face of the planet. Given these tendencies, it is not difficult to understand why American TV, and increasingly all of American society, has become a veritable laboratory and playground for the ceaseless production of images that deliberately confuse and blur the lines between what's real and what's artificial.[9]

---

7. Richard Schickel, *Intimate Strangers, The Culture of Celebrity, How Our National Obsession With Celebrity Shapes Our Worlds and Bends Our Minds*. Garden City, NY: Doubleday & Company, 1985.
8. Stuart Ewen, *All Consuming Images, The Politics of Style in Contemporary Culture*. New York: Basic Books, 1988, p. 22.
9. *Ibid.*

For all practical purposes, everything in U.S. society has become a branch of entertainment: business, news, politics, religion, you name it. Why? When people no longer can make sense of the world because of either its sheer complexity, or the overall volume of supposed "information" with which we are bombarded daily, then they will seek coherency elsewhere. They will find it in the endless pursuit of nonstop, disconnected sights, sounds, images, and pleasing personalities that pretend to offer them coherence. As a result, we no longer prefer to confront reality directly, for long ago we learned and accepted the fact that reality has for all practical purposes become unmanageable. Instead, we have turned our energies to the proliferation, production, and consumption of endless amounts of unreality to soothe our tired and fractured egos.

While TV is of course not the only factor that is responsible, we should also make no mistake about its immense power. Indeed, TV may in fact be *the prime culprit*. It has become the very model by which we frame nearly everything in American society. Everything now imitates and/or caricatures TV as TV itself caricatures and/or imitates everything else. We have newspapers, magazines, and even "books" in the form of TV screens or TV reality. (That is, TV like all media does not merely portray the world "as it is" but instead "constructs it" according to its own particular rules.[10]) For instance, *USA Today*, the newspaper, is a simulation of "TV news" that is itself a simulation of "real news." And "USA Today on TV" is a simulation of *USA Today*, the newspaper. At each step in the chain, we recede further and further from reality. Conversely, each step heightens a felt sense of unreality. We have so thoroughly merged symbols, information, and entertainment that few of us can distinguish between them anymore.

A recent poll by the Times-Mirror organization lends some support to these notions [see Box 2]. Apparently, when asked, up to 50 percent of those who watch so-called "reality" or crime re-creation TV shows such as "Rescue 911" felt that they were watching the "real thing" *even when there was a clear statement at the bottom of the TV screen that the scene was a reenactment or re-creation of a supposedly real crime*. Things have indeed reached a real low when

10. See E. Ann Kaplan, *Rocking Around the Clock, Music Television, Post-Modernism, and Consumer Culture*. New York: Routledge, 1987.

people either cannot or no longer wish to differentiate between "reality" and "unreality."

The reasons are not hard to fathom. When increasingly *all* shows on TV either look alike or strive to have the same look, then why indeed should anyone be able to differentiate between what's news, advertising, entertainment, sports, and even politics? If anything, the growing inability to discriminate between different types of programs demonstrates just how "eminently successful" TV has become in obliterating the ability to think, to handle complexity in a world that is more complex than ever. The success of TV may be measured by the fact that it has produced a critical mass of programs that essentially all look alike. The consequence is the achievement of a critical saturation point [see Box 3]. *For this reason, no individual show or program, no matter how excellent it may be on its own, can be evaluated independently of the larger pattern or context within which all shows operate.* TV must be approached and understood as a *total stream of consciousness* into which all shows are absorbed as part of an unfolding spectacle. The failure to see this and to appreciate this larger pattern is a primary example of the Fragmentation and Buffering games we described earlier. Without this broader appreciation, one reaches erroneous conclusions as to the full effects of TV in U.S. society.

American TV is fundamentally an extension of a consumerist society. As such, its prime purpose is not to entertain but to sell goods [see Box 4]. It is easier to accomplish this if one has an audience that is not only passive but uneducated and further which has been conditioned to believe that one's success in life depends on buying the right things. Given the dominant tendency of Americans to purchase all kinds of external objects to solve their most basic problems, it is not surprising that alcohol and drug addiction are so high in U.S. society. Indeed, the best estimates are that the U.S. consumes some 80 percent of the world's supply of cocaine. If it's okay to buy certain products to feel beautiful, then why isn't it just as "okay" to buy drugs to deaden pain? In fact, hasn't the American public gotten the true message, namely, "Just say yes to consumption!"

The principal characteristics of the Unreality game are precisely those factors responsible for the creation of unreality:

(1) the widespread adoption and uncritical acceptance of TV as the model or standard for the portrayal of reality throughout all of American society;

(2) the infusion of entertainment into virtually every aspect of U.S. society;

(3) the relentless blurring of the lines between some of the most critical functions of society, e.g., the creation of "infotainment" through the unprincipled merging of news and entertainment;

(4) the growing ability via electronic means to make the unreal look as real as possible so that one either cannot differentiate between them or no longer cares to differentiate.[11]

To explore the phenomenon of unreality further, we need to examine some of the subgames that create as well as maintain it. While many of the games we have encountered previously apply here as well, what's interesting and important are the modifications that are introduced to the games when we are dealing at the level of society. Equally important and striking are the extreme interconnections that exist between the games at this level as well.

1. The "Entertainment" Game

The primary purpose of the Entertainment game is to divert us as a society from facing painful facts, such as the U.S. now lives in a world that it no longer controls to the degree it once did. The purpose of this game is also to sustain the primary myths upon which U.S. society was founded and thereby perpetuate the illusions that the myths still apply in their original version without substantial modification, abandonment or their replacement by new ones that are better suited to a new world. The motivation behind the entertainment game also stems from incapacity of many in our society (including those in other societies as well) to sustain conflict [see Box 5]. In this sense, the

---

11. More than anyone, we appreciate that a precise definition of unreality would be of enormous help. Unfortunately, it is not possible to give one because of the extreme fluidity and complexity of the concept. Nonetheless, we can give a "sense" of the term. The term "unreal" or "unreality" is used in a number of distinct and yet interrelated senses: (1) the *naturally occurring* appearance of a physical phenomenon (or a person, car, etc.), such as a sunset which is so striking in its colors, beauty, setting, etc., that it is both experienced and described as "unreal" because it represents an extreme as measured along some scale typically connoting perfection, beauty, etc.; (2) the *deliberate as well as unintended creation* by humans of a scene, object, work of art, etc., so striking or beautiful that it is experienced or described as "unreal" because it represents the extreme magnification of properties that are only found in their "lesser condition or original state" in nature; (3) the *creation* primarily through the medium of entertainment of a work, a show, a performance, etc., that has the effect of denying the complexity of the surrounding environment, i.e, of rendering the world far simpler than it actually is; and, (4) the features of all those new environments to which we are not yet adapted and hence do not yet accept as "normal."

Entertainment game is a close replica of the Buddies and Be Nice to People games that we described earlier, only in the current case the Entertainment game now applies to the level of society considered as a whole. From this perspective, Ronald Reagan's immense popularity was due to the fact that he represented the ultimate "good buddy, daddy, or favorite uncle" whom all of us could identify with and trust implicitly even if many of us didn't like his policies. In addition, the Entertainment game adds another dimension. It appeals to the growing incapacity of many in our society to tolerate and to appreciate complexity as well as conflict. Thus, the Entertainment game perpetuates the fantasy of an earlier, simpler, kinder, gentler era in which America was firmly in control as well as on top. It represents an age where every day is literally "a new morning in America."

As no one should be fooled by the apparent surface benignness or banality of the Buddies and the Be Nice to People games, no one should be fooled by the apparent surface benignness of the Entertainment game as well. As Aldous Huxley in particular warned,[12] the greatest danger to Western societies did not arise from external threats as posed, say, by totalitarian governments—what Robert Reich has called the Mob at the Gates—but rather it arose from their own internal addiction to the overwhelming volumes of banality that they produced themselves. This banality is not only subsumed under the Entertainment game, but more specifically, we refer to it as the Rot from Within in order to contrast it with Reich's Rot at the Top. As such, the Rot from Within has close affinities with what Wilkinson has labeled the Fear of Falling Away and the Fear of Falling Apart.

On its surface the Entertainment game appears so harmless, which is precisely why it posed such a great and serious threat to Huxley and to others such as Neil Postman. It poses a serious threat precisely because it is not even recognized as a "threat" per se.

The Entertainment game can be seen in the relentless blurring of boundaries that occurs on TV in particular and increasingly in every dimension of U.S. society. For instance, a growing number of observers and critics of TV have complained strongly with regard to the crossover or infusion of entertainment into TV news and so-called reality crime shows, or more generally, "reality re-creations/documentaries" [see Box 7]. They point out that the primary function of

12. See Neil Postman, *Amusing Ourselves to Death, Public Discourse in the Age of Show Business*. New York: Viking, 1985.

news, TV or otherwise, is not to entertain via cutesy personalities, the extreme intermingling and juxtaposition of the serious with the banal in a "rapid context of no context," and the use of dazzling and slick graphics. Instead, the fundamental purpose of news is to inform and to serve as the watchdog of society and its institutions. Why else indeed would the news as part of the fourth estate be accorded such fundamental protection under the U.S. Constitution? Surely, entertainment is not critical either to the functioning or to the existence of Western democracies.[13] Thus, entertainment per se is not to be accorded any special protection under the law. This does not mean that in order to perform its critical functions news thereby has to be inherently dull. It does mean that asking the question, "What's wrong with entertainment?" as Mitroff encountered repeatedly during the course of discussing his previous book, *The Unreality Industry*, is akin to asking the question, "What's wrong with dessert?" There's nothing wrong with either except of course when they become the main staple of one's diet.

One of the main dangers associated with the infusion of entertainment, especially into nearly every aspect of the society, is that entertainment—and not accuracy, importance, or truthfulness—becomes the norm, the standard of conducting all business. When this happens, one has to keep the audience continually stimulated. In the words of the entertainment business itself, one has to supply an emotional high or a "chill bump" every fifteen seconds or so in order to keep the audience entertained and ultimately hooked [see Box 8]. When entertainment becomes the norm, everything is sacrificed or becomes subservient to it. For example, during the reporting of the October 1989 San Francisco earthquake, not only were certain pictures shown over and over again—naturally the most vivid such as a car plummeting over the edge of the upper deck of the San Francisco-Oakland Bay Bridge—but Dan Rather in particular pulled out of one eyewitness the fact that he had seen "human brains splattered on the pavement." Everything, including disasters, is thus framed in terms of its entertainment—read "sensationalistic"—values. To repeat, the danger is that

---

13. We are well aware that there is indeed a sense in which entertainment is critical to every society in relieving tensions, providing relaxation, prompting creativity, etc. We are also well aware that entertainment, or more broadly aesthetics, is a critical element in everything that humans do. In saying that entertainment is not critical, we are objecting to the case where it threatens or has become the *dominant content* of activities such as news and science where supposedly entertainment is presumably only a servant.

TV news programs and especially re-creations are no longer done to the traditional standards of journalistic news reporting but rather to those of entertainment.[14] The real danger is that the public will neither appreciate this nor ultimately care.

Why should one any longer be surprised to find that up to 50 percent of those who view so-called "reality re-creations" such as "911" think they are seeing the "real thing" even when at the bottom of the screen is a "clear label" saying that what the viewer is watching is a "simulation or re-creation." Such ploys on the part of the producers would truly be laughable if they were not shameful, and did not border on the deliberately dishonest. When virtually all TV programs on virtually all channels use the same graphic effects—such as multiple colors, windows, slickness—when text and images are interspersed in such abundance, then why indeed should viewers either be able to or want to keep the various effects apart? *If TV and all of U.S. society are dominated by imagery, then why shouldn't words and text themselves now be regarded merely as images?*

It is as if our very brains were evolved to watch TV with its fast-paced, never-ending action shots. In the words of Jack Solomon, "Television, with its constant changes of scene, its rapid pacing, and almost infinite variety, is uniquely suited to satisfy our restless craving for sensory stimulation and change. It's almost as if we evolved to watch TV."[15] Is it really any wonder then why the average length of a political sound byte has fallen from approximately forty seconds in 1968 to under ten seconds in 1988? Is it any further surprise that in 1968 the presidential candidates uttered uninterrupted sound bytes that lasted for at least one minute some 25 percent of the time, but that this *never* occurred in 1988?[16]

As we have already seen and as we shall explore further, the Entertainment game bears strong relations to the Reality Blurring game by radically smudging the lines between what's news and what's enter-

14. We harbor no illusions that the news has ever been free of sensationalism or entertainment. For an interesting discussion of the history of news, particularly how it has always been in line with sensationalism, see Mitchell Stephens, *A History of News, From the Drum to the Satellite*. New York: Viking, 1988. We are thereby not assuming that there was some golden age of news whereby it was untainted by corrupting influences. Rather, what we feel is different is the total pervasiveness, the "total surround" of a medium such as TV which is not only omnipresent but ever-present. This is what seems to us to be so different about today's environment.

15. Jack Solomon, *The Signs of Our Times*, Los Angeles: Jeremy Tarcher, Inc., 1988, p. 125.

16. These data are taken from various newspaper reports of a study published by the Kennedy School of Government at Harvard University in 1990.

tainment, between what's real live footage, and what's staged or re-created, etc. As such, the Entertainment and Reality Blurring games stand in marked contrast to the Fragmentation and Buffering games that we described earlier. While the primary purpose of the Fragmen-tation and Buffering games is to block off or to shield from one an-other the various aspects of a complex world that now impact on one another so strongly that their extreme separation no longer makes any sense. The purpose of the Entertainment and Reality Blurring games is to throw together the most disparate, nonsensical aspects of a complex reality in virtually no discernible pattern at all, in what may be called "a pattern of no pattern." But herein lies a supreme irony.

When it is in the interests of the media and business powers that be, they are perfectly capable of switching from (1) the Fragmentation and Buffering games to (2) the Entertainment and Reality Blurring games! However, the nature and quality of the switch is as remarkable and important as the very fact of the switch itself. Both cases are guided largely by forces that are unconscious. In the one case, there is a radical fragmentation of reality because of the philosophy of nature which we inherited largely from the British. This philosophy goes un-der the general name of British empiricism. In this sense, neither Reich nor Wilkinson have identified the full set of myths, fears, or potent forces acting on American culture. In the metaphysic of British empiricism, reality literally is that which is composed of or can be decomposed into separate atoms, i.e., autonomous self-existing units of reality. In the other case, there is radical blurring or extreme mixing of things because we have neither inherited nor developed a metaphy-sic based on the relations or interconnectedness between things. Thus, one oscillates between (1) the most radical decomposition of things wherein nearly all meaning is lost, and (2) the most radical mixing where as a result things make no sense because not only is there a lack of a coherent pattern, but the radical mixing process itself is bent on destroying all sensible patterns.

As is so often the case, the greatest poets are capable of capturing and expressing this better in one line than all the prose in the world. Thus, T.S. Eliot has written with characteristic acuity, "Humankind cannot bear very much reality," except of course when it is in the interest of big media and big business to deliberately orchestrate real-ity to their tune. And big business it is indeed. In 1988, the U.S. entertainment industry brought in some $5.5 billion in *foreign earn-*

ings. Behind the aerospace industry, the entertainment industry was the U.S.'s second largest net exporter. Apparently, the rest of the planet likes our brand of entertainment or unreality as well.

2. The Celebrity Game

Richard Schickel[17] may have gotten to the core of this game better than anyone else through his acute observation that "in contemporary America, one is either a celebrity or one is nothing at all."

Two questions in particular confront anyone who attempts to deal with the problem of celebrityhood in present-day America: (1) What are the critical functions that celebrities serve, and hence, what are the reasons for their existence? (2) Why is America in particular especially attracted to—or better yet, addicted to—celebrities? The first question is almost trivial. Celebrities are the projective totems and icons of society writ large. They exist in order to satisfy the most basic psychological needs. For the general populace—whose lives are filled increasingly with the pain of acute boredom, frustration, hopelessness, an overwhelming sense of dread, overpowering feelings of anxiety, and impotence in the face of monumental social ills (such as a rapidly deteriorating economy, educational system, infrastructure, and a greatly diminished sense of power)—celebrities offer one of the quickest and most effective ways out. Even more fundamental, in a world where the existence of one's basic sense of "self" is threatened, celebrities allow us a distinctively unique way to feel alive and, even more basic, literally "to be":

> . . . If great art loses its aura in the marketplace of mass impression, the individual life of the celebrity achieves an aura through mass reproduction. In their ability to magnify, and to create near universal recognition, the mass media are able to invest the everyday lives of formerly everyday people with a magical sense of value, a secularized imprint of the *sacred* [emphasis in original]. . .

Celebrities, though they shine above us, are also—many of them—very much like us. Identification is easy. The whole story of their success is that they came from "the mass." They were once unknown. In a society where conditions of anonymity fertil-

17. Schickel, *op. cit.*

ize the desire "to be somebody," the *dream of identity*, the *dream of wholeness* [emphasis in original], is intimately woven together with the desire to be known; to be visible; to be documented, for all to see.

Previously unknown, the celebrity was often also previously poor. The combination of anonymity and poverty are often ritually linked in the telling of a success story . . . .

Celebrity forms a symbolic pathway, connecting each aspiring individual to a universal image of fulfillment: to be someone, when "being no one" is the norm.[18]

Celebrities exist so that we can project our inner needs and fantasies for unlimited power, love, beauty, adoration, wealth, fame, onto human gods. Through celebrities we attain what we are not able to experience or to have in our daily lives. In short, they fill up what in earlier chapters we referred to as the fragile inner sense of "self" of those whose personalities are poorly or weakly developed.[19] Celebrities are not only master players but representatives of all the Image games we encountered earlier (e.g., the I Should Always Look Good and the Magician's games among others). This is their fundamental purpose. The unwritten, but nonetheless strictly understood, social contract existing between us and our celebrities is that they are to satisfy our basic needs, conscious as well as unconscious, for engaging in Image games.

There are of course other critical functions that are also well understood and accepted that they are expected to satisfy. For instance, it is not only expected, but in some cases virtually demanded that celebrities engage in the Razor's Edge game. Thus, through celebrities we not only live out our most grandiose fantasies, but also our barely repressed desires to engage in socially undesirable and destructive acts such as embezzlement, suicide, illicit sex (e.g., l'affair Rob Lowe), and even murder. We protest that they must be punished for their outrageousness, but unconsciously it is an entirely different matter. We both identify with them and applaud them. Indeed, we gloat when *they* are able to thumb their noses as well as their other body parts at the system. As much as we want our stars and celebrities to tumble, for

18. Ewen, *op. cit.* pp. 93-96.
19. J. Martin, *Who Am I This Time? Uncovering the Fictive Personality*. New York: Norton, 1988.

great falls are also part of the game itself, we want everything about them to be monumentally outrageous. We need our Leonas and Zsa Zsas to love-hate much as we once did our mommies and daddies.

A new aspect of celebrityhood that has only been made possible with the technology of the 20th and 21st centuries is especially disturbing and ominous. It is a fascinating dual-edged phenomenon or aspect of celebrityhood. On the one hand, because celebrities are more widely viewed by a mass audience than ever before in human history, their "shelf life" or "staying power" so to speak is shorter than ever. Thus, the need to constantly manufacture new celebrities and remanufacture or retrofit old ones is greater than ever. Because there are so many more outlets or channels in which to observe celebrities, we consume them at a greater and faster rate. For instance, MTV features some 2,000 four-minute rock videos every week.[20] While no one watches all 2,000, continual watching is not necessary in order for constant consumption to occur. If MTV is indeed akin to a continual flow of uninterrupted, primal-like images, then it is only necessary to dip in every so often in order to experience the sense of the total flow. From this perspective, it is no longer necessary to watch the whole phenomenon in order to experience the whole. It is as if MTV were a gigantic hologram where the part is in the whole and the whole is in the part. But if so, then the pressure on rock video stars to continually keep abreast and change their images is enormous. A star can and must undergo as many as three to four transformations per year in order to keep current. The constant redefining and re-creation of one's image is both ruthless and relentless.

On the other hand, modern technology has also made it possible for a star such as Elvis, whose fame has only continued to grow since his death, to live forever. In many senses, an untimely or early death of a superstar like a James Dean is one of the best possible devices for insuring immortality. In Elvis's case, it is reputed that the "electronic rights" to his persona or image are owned by a media company in L.A. Current technology is still too crude to produce an electronic image that is so lifelike that one could no longer tell whether it was originally created by a computer or produced by an actual camera shot of the original person. The eventual goal, however, is to produce a computer-generated electronic image that is so lifelike that the possibility of differentiating between them will be virtually impossible.

20. E. Ann Kaplan, *op. cit.*

When this happens, then Elvis will truly live forever, but not in the ways that so many of his zanier fans think! When the computer image of Elvis becomes as good as or even better than the original, then it will be possible to put the electronic Elvis into an unlimited number of new TV shows, movies, etc.

The adoration or consumption of celebrities is especially pronounced in Western democratic societies. Lacking a true and indigenous royalty, celebrities have come to serve many of the same functions as royalty once did. In addition, societies such as the U.S. are especially prone to celebrity creation and worship. America is a profoundly anti-intellectual society whose distrust of intellectuals goes far back and is thus deeply rooted in our history [see Box 6]. The distrust of intellectuals is part of Reich's myth of the Rot at the Top. True, America was founded on ideas that were the creation of men who were as intellectually capable as any the world has ever seen, but from its very beginnings, America has revered the common man, and not the person of ideas or ideas themselves. In addition, perhaps no other society has celebrated the notion of the self-made or self-created person. Lacking therefore a fundamental belief in either ideas or intellectuals, America has always turned her energies to other sources such as con artists, pretty faces, pleasing personalities as well as characters of all kinds in order to signify the importance or significance of something.[21] In this sense, the current preoccupation with TV anchors is only the latest in this long trend.

Lacking the ability, plus clear-cut standards themselves, to judge ideas and things in terms of their inherent qualities or merits, is it any wonder that a growing body of uneducated people would judge things based mainly on their superficial qualities? Is it really any wonder why TV anchors would have become and have needed to become celebrities themselves so that they now overshadow the "news" they deliver? As part of a never-ending stream of unrelated, virtually meaningless images and pseudo events that they themselves help to create, is it again any wonder that they too have become largely images to be consumed? [see Box 10]. In a world that has become inordinately sophisticated in the elaborate production and consumption of images,[22] it is no longer surprising that the superstar TV anchors must appear at

21. Braudy, op. cit.
22. Irving Rein et al., High Visibility: How Executives, Politicians, Entertainers, Athletes, and Other Professionals Create, Market, and Achieve Successful Images. New York: Dodd, Mead & Company, 1987.

"important events" such as the tearing down of the Berlin Wall in order to signify its "true" importance.

In a society that is addicted to all kinds of substances, and further, one that because of its inherent narcissism believes that it is entitled to do so, why shouldn't it have an addiction to celebrities as well? Is there not in fact an uncanny correlation between a society's huge consumption of cocaine and celebrities and its inordinately high consumption of the world's energy supply? After all, aren't we mandated to consume?

If we are indeed so mandated to consume, then celebrities are in effect our ultimate consumables. Herein, however, lies a supreme irony:

> Celebrities, collectively, supply us with the most accessible vision of what wealth means. Yet while their lives provide a vernacular depiction of *wealth* [emphasis in original], they also tend to mask the relationship between wealth and power. Though celebrities are routinely described as "fabulously wealthy," they are linked to their audiences by the fact that for both consumption serves as the primary expression of their power, or lack of it. True, celebrities can go to the movies without having to wait in line, and can get the best table in the house at a moment's notice. Yet these are essentially consumer aspirations; to purchase without restraint, to enjoy the envious glances of those around them. In critical ways, however, most celebrities stand in a similar relation to meaningful, decision making power over society as do the "unknown" people who admire them:
> Few celebrities are the ones "who really run things. . . ."
> As consumers, most celebrities are also *employees* [emphasis in original]. Their value, their celebrity itself, is sold "piecemeal," like a "commodity." Their fame and their fortune is "exposed to all the vicissitudes of competition, to all the fluctuations of the market. . . ."
> In this sense, although their pay is enough to make them the uncontested "aristocracy of labor," their exploitation, their status as commodities, is more visible than in other areas of employment. They, literally are the commodities being sold; fabricated, most of the time, on an elaborate, cultural assembly line.
> It is this objectivication of the person that, most probably,

explains much of the turmoil and grief, the identity crisis that
often accompanies stardom. Perhaps celebrities, too, have become uncomfortable in their own skin as they, in the eyes of
others, become frozen images; as their faces and bodies and
mannerisms become icons; always the personage, never the person. It is difficult to be a disembodied image.

Celebrities last as long as the people continue buying. If a
celebrity declines—as it often does—they become parts of an
enormous, cultural garbage pile; worthless, forgotten, or re-
tained in the mind as pieces of trivia. It is on this level, as they
are faithfully kept in the popular memory, that the link between
the known and the unknown is most poignant.[23]

3. The Technophilia Game

The Elvis phenomenon we described in the immediately preceding game is symptomatic of the Technophilia game. The purposes of
this game are manifold: (1) to assert continually our mastery over the
world; (2) to divert negative feelings and energy (e.g., boredom) from
the Razor's Edge game into supposedly worthwhile ends (e.g., national defense); and (3) to avoid facing dread (e.g., one's mortality).
According to the distinguished historian Daniel Boorstin,[24] it was no
random accident at all that the U.S. was quicker than almost any other
society in human history to adopt technology on a mass scale and to
weave it into virtually every aspect of its life. The supreme irony is
that the very technologies that the U.S. so quickly and thoroughly
adopted because of the incredible emphasis that the U.S. placed on
such values as continual innovation and individualism actually contributed to their erosion. The widespread adoption and infusion of the
machine into every aspect and fiber of American society actually led to
the decline and suppression of both individualism and innovation. The
U.S. today represents largely a parody of individualism.[25] It is one of
the most conformist societies on the face of the planet. We proclaim
loudly and constantly our individualism en masse, so to speak. How-

23. Ewen, *op. cit.* pp. 100-101.
24. Daniel J. Boorstin, *Hidden History, Exploring Our Secret Past.* New York: Vintage Books,
    1989; see also Daniel J. Boorstin, *The Americans: The Democratic Experience.* New York:
    Vintage Books, 1974.
25. Robert N. Bellah et al., *Habits of the Heart, Individualism and Commitment in American
    Life.* Berkeley, CA: University of California Press, 1985.

ever, when such words have largely become advertising symbols for watches, cigarettes, and even political campaigns, then they have virtually lost their meaning. Thus, for example, the word "citizen" has become appropriated as the brand name of a watch. For another, the word "truth" has become the name of a particular brand of cigarettes.

What is especially disturbing is the gap that has grown between our attitudes toward technology and people. Although our attitudes regarding technology are decidedly mixed—we both revere and fear it, praise and condemn it at the very same time—our feelings toward technology contain many of the very same projections that we once harbored exclusively for human beings. It is of course no contradiction to say that we both revere technology and people. The point is that the people we now revere are like our technology mostly human creations, i.e., celebrities. What's absent is the reverence for true heroes because we can no longer distinguish them from false creations. Thus, as our disappointment and distrust have grown with respect to ourselves in general and our leaders in particular, we have transferred onto our marvelous electronic machines the qualities we once reserved for ourselves and the gods. Look at the messages that are sent constantly to our youngest via the medium of TV. The Saturday morning so-called "children's TV shows" present episode after episode wherein pure electronic and half-human, half-machine hybrids are the heroes. In nearly every case, it is the machines that are the smarter, braver, more intelligent, and better than their human counterparts.

4. The Radical Blurring/Fragmentation/Buffering and Blaming Games

On every aspect and front of our existence, physical as well as mental, we have so thoroughly blurred and mixed the elements of reality and unreality together that it has not only become impossible to say which is which but the very distinction may be dead for all practical purposes [see Boxes 9 and 10]. The radical blurring of our physical and mental realms is one of the most important and critical aspects of the Radical Blurring game that we need to explore. However, before we do so, we need to explore the counterparts to the Blurring game, the forms of the Fragmentation/Buffering/Blaming games that are played at the societal level. We have grouped all these together and have chosen to discuss all of these seemingly disparate games in order to demonstrate the strong connectedness that exists between them.

If the lines between nearly every conceivable aspect of our environment, both physical and mental, either have become or are in the process of becoming radically blurred, then some of the major rationalizations or defenses by which the TV and other media industries have defended themselves are invalid at best. At worst, they represent outright demagoguery. Again and again one encounters six principal arguments that those who work in virtually all media use to defend what they do. Not so surprisingly, these arguments are used much more frequently and with greater strength by those who work in TV and radio than by those who work in the print media, although to be sure they can be found even there [see Boxes 11, 12, and 13].

The six arguments are:

(1) The people themselves are largely to blame for what they get; in other words, this is the Grand Stupidity Thesis. The people deserve what they get because they are inordinately and inherently stupid.

(2) We only give the people what they want.

(3) If people don't like what they see or what they listen to, then they can either turn off their sets or switch channels.

(4) What's wrong after all with entertainment?

(5) If we don't give people what they want, then somebody else will.

(6) People can differentiate between what's "hard or real news" and what's entertainment.

Given the tremendous power of the media, each argument is used to buffer the proponents from the tremendous responsibilities that accompany such power. Let us consider each of these critical arguments in turn.

It is undoubtedly true that the public itself ultimately must accept a large part of the blame for the dreadful state of American TV. It is indeed true that American TV could not survive, let alone prosper, if there were not a significant audience for it. However, even if the Stupidity Thesis were true in its entirety, this does not excuse or relieve the media from their responsibilities. What the media all too conveniently ignore in the equation is that they are fundamentally responsible not only for feeding on this "stupidity" but of further encouraging it to the benefit of their huge profits. To say that the public is solely responsible for its own stupidity is to ignore the *symbiotic* relationship that exists between those who are supposedly stupid and those who feed and profit from it. Even more, it is to ignore the tremendous role that the media have in both creating and furthering such stupidity. It is also to ignore, by not examining, the moral or ethical principles upon which the behavior and the policies of the media rest. Just stating the major moral principle is enough to see how utterly ridiculous it is. It reads as follows: "Whenever a segment of the public exists (and of course, the bigger the better it is) that is stupid enough to consume whatever we produce, then we are justified morally in satisfying that need or demand." This is the great moral base upon which the media in our society currently rest.

The second argument, "We only give the people what they want," is the argument of the drug dealer and pornographer. First of all, leaving aside its moral implications, the argument itself is only partly true at best. If the media were indeed giving the people what they truly want, then why do new network shows fail at an alarmingly high rate? The media themselves, especially TV, are more than willing to admit that they can't predict the taste of the public. That is precisely one of the reasons why so many shows ape one another. The point is that one cannot truly have it both ways. One cannot argue that one is giving the public what they want when so much of what is presented fails spectacularly. Be this as it may, more important is the notion that the media *only fulfill* an already existing demand and do not, like the drug dealer, participate in the creation and maintenance of the demand itself. This not only conveniently ignores the symbiotic relationship that always exists between the producer and the buyer of a product or service, but it also ignores the differential power of the media in creating, maintaining, and shaping needs themselves.

No matter what field of human endeavor one investigates, one knows that one has indeed reached moral rock bottom whenever a party defends what they do in terms of "We only give them what they want." Surely, if one had a better, stronger moral principle to trot out, one would surely trot it out at such a time in order to defend one's activities. The fact that the media repeatedly fall back on such a line of reasoning or argument in order to justify what they do shows how incredibly shaky is the moral foundation upon which they stand.

A third argument, "If people don't like what they are getting, then they can always turn off their sets or switch channels," is especially interesting. This argument is symptomatic of either (a) the outright refusal of the media to recognize the full nature of their impacts, (b) their inability to do so, (c) their ignorance of them, and/or (d) all of the above. Whatever the true case, this particular argument may be the most demagogic of all.

If TV, through the general and widespread adoption of its general format and look by such newspapers as *USA Today* and magazines such as *Business Week*, has insinuated itself so thoroughly throughout our entire culture, then the argument that "if you don't like what you see and hear, either turn it off or switch" is truly preposterous. *It refuses to recognize let alone understand that it is truly impossible to turn off a whole culture!* It just can't be done. *One can physically turn off a set, but one cannot turn off its effects if they are so deeply embedded thoughout an entire culture.* It may be comforting to believe that by physically turning off a dial or a switch that one still had independence and freedom of thought and action, but such thoughts and actions are largely symbolic gestures devoid of any true significance [see Box 14].

The third argument also ignores conveniently that if increasingly everything on TV—whether on public, commercial, cable, or special access channels—looks alike, then the proliferation in the number of channels is not equivalent to the increase in the real quality of choice. The argument not only confuses *quantity* of choice with *quality*, but deliberately hides and obscures the fact that the illusion of choice is precisely that, largely an illusion. The sad fact is that in its constant endless battle to raise funding, public TV is being forced to adopt many of the same techniques and formats as that of commercial TV. Here again, the players of the Buffering game would have us believe that public TV can remain off by itself in some protected realm and be uninfluenced by all that is taking place around us.

The fourth argument, "What's wrong with entertainment?" is akin, as we noted earlier, to the question "What's wrong with dessert?" The answer of course is "Nothing, except when it becomes the whole meal itself." A society that has become so addicted to dessert, froth, and entertainment in order to function is not exactly a society that is prepared to face hard realities, let alone change in order to meet them.

The fifth argument, "If we don't do it, then someone else will," is also pathetic from a moral standpoint. The moral translation of this argument is: *"Whenever there exists at least one other party in the world willing to commit an evil, whether for profit or not, then one is justified, if not warranted, in committing that evil oneself."* Expressed in this form, the principle is too outrageous to warrant analysis, except of course that which is already contained in this brief sentence itself.

We will not bother to comment on the sixth argument since we have already done so before. Although we unfortunately lack the data that could conclusively prove the case one way or another, we have already observed from a previous study that at least up to 50 percent of people who watch so-called crime or reality re-creation shows cannot differentiate.

At their heart, all Buffering and Fragmentation games rest on their unwillingness or inability to face the fact that we live in a world that is interconnected in every conceivable dimension. Thus, unlike earlier, simpler eras where reality could be broken down into relatively stable, independent parts—much like a big machine can be decomposed into its separate, autonomous parts—this cannot be done in a world where everything is part of a highly interconnected, electronic system. The definition of a system is precisely that of an entity for which its various subparts neither have a separate existence nor function apart from the larger whole in which they reside. For instance, the human heart, lungs, eyes neither exist nor function *completely* outside of the whole system, the whole human being, of which they are merely parts.

To show how important it is to attack head-on the inappropriateness of the Buffering and Fragmentation games, it is enough to consider that TV may be the "true" educational system of the U.S. Surely no one can argue that TV is not one of the major reflectors, if not creators, of the value system of U.S. society. The fact that American children are exposed to so many hours of TV with its constant bombardment of images may be enough to support the contention that TV is indeed one of the major educational delivery systems in our society. If this is indeed the case, then an interesting attack on the Buffering and Fragmentation games is as follows.

Apparently, every evening the New York Life Insurance Company completely flies all of its billings to Ireland. This is not primarily because wage rates are cheaper in Ireland, which indeed they are, but because New York Life cannot find enough trained workers to read the company's billings and process them into a computer. Lacking the presence of a trained work force, it is cheaper for New York Life to fly all of its billings to Ireland, than to try to correct the defects of an untrained, uneducated work force. If this is indeed the case, then it makes a mockery of many of the proposals that have been put forth by American business leaders in order to correct the ills of our educational system. It is all right, and indeed even necessary, for business leaders such as David Kerns,[26] president of Xerox, to argue that the U.S. must put its incredible resources behind teachers. We must also become a society that truly celebrates and rewards excellence.

All this is fine and to be applauded. However, what this so conveniently ignores is that many of the very businesses that complain so loudly that they cannot find enough trained workers who are capable enough to follow the complex directions needed to produce goods that can compete in a global economy are some of the very same businesses that sponsor so much of what we see on television. The point is that the Buffering and Fragmentation games truly allow a large and complex society such as ours not to see and not to know what their respective "right and left hands" are doing. If big business thinks that it can sponsor all kinds of trivial and junk TV and then turn around and put the burden for correcting this solely on the education system, then it is truly dumber than many of us already believe it is. This very point was nicely expressed in a letter to the editor of *U.S. News & World Report* [see Box 15].

26. David T. Kerns and Denis P. Doyle, *Winning the Brain Race, A Bold Plan to Make Our Schools Competitive*. San Francisco: ICS Press, 1989.

Chapter 9

Cosmic Technophilia

. . . In our modern world there are philosophers and psychologists who maintain that this human consciousness of ours is an item that can be dispensed with . . .

William Barrett,
The Death of the Soul,
Tinker Press, New York, 1986, p. xii

. . . Contemporary society, so inundated by unreal images of itself in the media, and scientific classifications, in advertising, not only has come to believe in the reality of those images, but has actually become those images. Indistinguishable from its own illusions, contemporary society is now through and through a fake. Self-deceptive as well, it has constructed certain places as official illusions in order to deny its own unreality. Disneyland is one such place.

[Jean Baudrillard] writes: "Disneyland is there to conceal the fact that it is the 'real' country, all of 'real' America which *is* Disneyland. . . ." Disneyland is presented as imaginary in order to make us believe that the rest is real, when in fact all of Los Angeles and the America surrounding it are no longer real, but of the order of the hyper-real and of simulation.

Another way to explain the concept is the story of the Tasaday, people untouched by modern culture until their discovery in the '60s by anthropologists. . . . In 1971 the Philippine government decided to return the dying Tasaday to the jungle. There they were sealed off from tourists, anthropologists, colonists. But in doing this, Baudrillard argues, the government turned real primitives, who had already been changed by the experience in civilization, into simulated ones. Now they are locked into the jungle like so many "wild" specimens at the San Diego Wild Animal Park, merely to prove that the "real" primitives exist.

We are all Tasaday now [emphasis in original], Baudrillard believes. We are all simulated specimens "catalogued, and analyzed, and then artificially revived as though real." And America is the simulation capital of the world. That's why Baudrillard, who has been coming to Southern California to lecture since 1975, wanted to write a book about it. "The fascination of America," he says, "was that here was a fictional universe completely synchronous with my theory."

Annette Leddy,
"How Do You Explain America?"
Los Angeles Reader,
June 2, 1989, pp. 8-11.

We have tried throughout this book to understand the forces that produce crises in individuals, organizations, and societies. Our principal contention has been that major crises are essentially the result of disturbed games that individuals, organizations, and even whole societies get trapped into playing. From this perspective, there is a remarkable similarity between the different levels of society. This does not deny that in spite of this similarity the games we have observed are the result of very different forces.

This is also not to deny, on the surface at least, that there are vast differences between crises of the kind and magnitude of a Three Mile Island which pose severe threats to the physical environment and those by the electronic media which pose a threat to the mental environment. And yet, as dissimilar as these first appear, the common thread or link between all crises, no matter at which level of society they appear, is the increasing role played by technology, on the one hand, and the growing incapacity or inability of people and institutions to manage technology on the other. Technology is not only increasingly a dominant force in every aspect of our society but it is transforming us faster than the social mechanisms of society can keep pace.

One can conceive of the games that are played at each level of society as the resultant outcome of the struggle or battle between two opposing forces: sustaining versus restraining. The sustaining or driving forces are those which are operating to produce and to maintain the games, and of course, the crises to which they must eventually lead. The restraining forces on the other hand are those which are acting to negate, to oppose, and to reduce the effects of the games.

The notion of driving versus restraining or opposing forces, as simplistic as it may be, is helpful nonetheless in comprehending phenomena that by any means are extremely difficult to grasp. Let us use then the idea of driving versus restraining forces to review and to summarize briefly our main results, and then to assess the prospects, if any, for reversing their most negative aspects.

In the previous chapter, we concluded that the Unreality Game is the result of some major driving forces in American culture and history: the radical blurring of the boundaries between physical and mental spaces, sex roles, news and entertainment (if not all information in general); the lack of a stable, fixed self; the breakdown of nearly all traditional institutions; the serious drop in voter turnout for U.S. national elections; the continually eroding trust in national elected leaders and institutions; the growing and deepening cynicism on the part of the public with regard to nearly all facets of U.S. life[1]; a culture that on its surface is the most technologically advanced on the face of the planet, but, as the highly controversial and perceptive French social critic Jean Baudrillard has observed, is, at its base, incredibly primitive:

> Deep down, the U.S., with its space, its technological refinement, its bluff good conscience, even in those spaces which it opens up for simulation, is the *only remaining primitive society* [emphasis in original]. The fascinating thing is to travel through it as though it were *the primitive society of the future* [emphasis ours], a society of complexity, hybridity, of the greatest intermingling, of a ritualism that is ferocious but whose superficial diversity lends it beauty, a society inhabited by a total metasocial fact with unforeseeable consequences, whose imminence is breathtaking, yet lacking a past through which to reflect on this, and

---

1. Donald L. Katner and Philip H. Mirvis, *The Cynical Americans, Living and Working in an Age of Discontent and Disillusion*, San Francisco: Jossey-Bass, 1989.

therefore fundamentally primitive. . . . Its primitivism has
passed into the hyperbolic, inhuman character of the universe
that is beyond us, that far outstrips its own moral, social, or
ecological rationale.[2]

Baudrillard's acute observations should not be dismissed easily.
Whether he is essentially correct or not (we believe he is) obscures an
important point. As we saw in earlier chapters, one of the single most
important things a major crisis does is to negate or to flip on its head
fundamental assumptions that were taken for granted prior to the crisis
itself. Baudrillard may indeed be wrong, but his acute observations
force us to examine seriously the possibility that one of the major
assumptions upon which U.S. society is built is fundamentally wrong:
The U.S. is *the most advanced society/civilization* on the face of the
planet. The counter-assumption is: The U.S. is *the most primitive society* of the future!

Baudrillard's is the peculiar kind of "wrongness" that is associated with genius. In the words of Kenneth Boulding, "It is the mark of
genius to hit big nails not squarely on their head." Although Boulding
did not state it, the converse proposition is equally true: It is the mark
of small minds to hit small nails squarely on the head. In this sense,
Baudrillard is akin to a Freud and to a Jung. It is not required that
Freud or Jung be entirely right or correct in every detail for us to
acknowledge the larger "truths" that both uncovered. Baudrillard may
be working precisely within the same kind of tradition.

The most general phenomenon, of which the Unreality Game is
only a partial reflection, is of course known by the label of post-modernism,[3] a particular term we happen to dislike because we believe it
misses an essential point. In the light of Baudrillard's observations
about the primitiveness of U.S. society, we believe a better term is
post-primitivism.

Baudrillard's analyses and contentions are exceedingly important
in illuminating the present condition of U.S. society. They are even
more important in illuminating the underlying driving forces responsible for the current state of U.S. society. What is so fascinating about

2. Jean Baudrillard, *America*, translated by Chris Turner, London: Verso, 1988, p. 7.
3. The concept of post-modernism refers to the radical mixing or presence of the most disparate
art forms, styles, modes of dress, etc., within the same setting or context. Post-modernism
thus challenges and breaks down, if not tramples upon, the walls or barriers between distinct
eras, styles, etc., that one would not have thought of transcending in earlier eras.

America is not only what it rejected from Europe, but what it accepted as well. If in the beginning we rejected vehemently (and the key thing here is the vehemence, i.e., the strength of the rejection) the divine right of kings to rule and to oppress us, we accepted just as strongly 18th century Europe's notion of progress. It was accepted however with a fundamental and significant twist or difference.

In the American context and experience, the proof of an idea lay in its material realization not in the mere abstract concept itself. America was not just a dream, a fantasy, but a *dream materialized*. The *possibility* of progress became a *mandate*, or a moral *imperative* for its achievement. In Baudrillard's words, America is "utopia achieved," i.e., a society where everything is possible and everything is available:

> We [Europeans] criticize Americans for not being able either to analyze or conceptualize. But this is a wrong-headed critique. It is we [Europeans] who imagine that everything culminates in transcendence, and that nothing exists which has not been conceptualized. Not only do [Americans] care little for such a view, but their perspective is the very opposite: It is not conceptualizing reality, but realizing concepts and materializing ideas, that interest them. The ideas of the religion and the light morality of the 18th century certainly, but also dreams, scientific values, and sexual perversions. Materializing freedom, but also the unconscious. Our fantasy is around space and fiction, but also our fantasy is sincerity and virtue, or our mad dreams of technicity. *Everything that has been dreamt on this side of the Atlantic has a chance of being realized on the other. They built the real out of ideas. We transform the real into ideas, or into ideology. Here in America only what is produced or manifested has meaning; for us in Europe only what can be thought or concealed has meaning. Even materialism is only an idea in Europe* [emphasis ours]. It is in America that it becomes concretely realized in the technical operation of things, and the transformation of a way of thinking into a way of life, in the "action" of life ("action" in the filmmaking sense, is what happens when the cameras begin to roll). For the materiality of things is, of course, their cinematography. *Americans believe in facts, but not in facticity* [i.e., the "concept" of "facts"] [emphasis ours]. They do not know that

facts are factitious, as their name suggests. It is this belief in facts, in the total credibility of what is done or seen, in this pragmatic evidence of things and an accompanying contempt for what may be called appearances or the play of appearances—a face does not deceive, behavior does not deceive, scientific process does not deceive, nothing deceives, nothing is ambivalent (and at bottom this is true: nothing deceives, there are no lies, *there is only simulation* [emphasis in original], which is precisely the facticity of facts)—that the Americans are a true utopian society, and their religion of the *fait accompli* and the naivete of their deductions, and their ignorance of the evil genius of things. You have to be utopian to think that in a human order, of whatever nature, things can be as plain and straightforward as that . . .[4]

What is important to understand is that in accepting or embracing a philosophy of what Baudrillard has termed "radical materialism," America rejected both consciously and unconsciously European notions of culture. If at its fundamental base culture is the fundamental social mechanism by which people give order to the universe, then the vehement rejection of European culture implied a fundamental rejection of the basic conceptual categories by which Europeans gave order to their landscape. Thus, to cultured Europeans it would be virtually unthinkable to mix, in a shopping mall no less, the reality of different historical periods with what Baudrillard has termed simulations. The fact that even in Europe and Canada such mixing is beginning to occur does not invalidate Baudrillard's fundamental point. The "mixing" is a testimony to the raw primitive power of U.S. consumer culture, not to the inherent worthiness of the ideas underlying it [see Box 1].

The rejection of European culture was more than "mere rejection," i.e., mere opposition. Instead, it was an affirmation that the new, endless, unbounded landscape offered infinite room in which to experiment. Literally nothing was ruled off limits. Not only did America offer the possibility of experimenting with everything, but she constituted a *moral imperative* to experiment with everything including oneself. Here at least one was free from the tired, stuffy constraints and categories of the past.

4. Baudrillard, *op. cit.*, pp. 84-85.

The distinguished anthropologist Edmund Leach[5] has written at length that it is the distinctively human invention of taboo that gives order to humankind's universe. For example, in every culture taboo marks off the boundaries between those animals that can be eaten and those that are to serve as household pets and presumably not to be consumed. The crucial point is that the taboos of different cultures often clash violently. This is why the experience of different cultures is itself often felt so violently. The devices that one culture uses to give order to its world often clash violently with those of another. Hence, the discomfort we often feel.

Baudrillard's point is that *from the standpoint of Europe, America has no culture*! This is not of course equivalent to saying that America has no rich and indigenous culture, which Baudrillard freely admits that it does. Rather, a society that is constituted on the basis of realizing utopia, if it is not already a "realized utopia," is one that is bent on "repealing all taboo," as crazy and as impossible as this may be. Thus, it is not that the U.S. literally has no culture, but that its own rich, indigenous culture is being cannibalized daily by what passes as culture, TV's "culture of simulation."

What many of those who were unsympathetic to Baudrillard's thesis apparently missed is that his critique of American culture (or its lack thereof) was also at the same time a powerful critique of European culture as well:

> There is no culture [in the U.S.], no cultural discourse. No ministries, no commissions, no subsidies, no promotion. There is none of the sickly cultural pathos which the whole of France indulges in, that fetishism of the cultural heritage, nor of our sentimental—and today also status and protectionist—invocation of culture. . . . not only does centralization not exist, but the idea of a cultivated culture does not exist either, no more than that of a theological, sacred religion. No culture of culture, no religion of religion, one should speak rather of an "anthropological" culture, which consists in the invention of mores and a way of life. That is the only interesting culture here, just as it is New York's streets and not its museums or galleries that are interesting. Even

---

5. Edmund Leach, "Anthropological Aspects of Language: Animal Categories and Verbal Abuse," in P. Marand (Ed.), *Mythology*. England: Penguin Books, 1973; see also, Edmund Leach, *Culture and Communication, The Logic by Which Symbols Are Connected*. New York: Cambridge University Press, 1976.

in dance, cinema, the novel, fiction, and architecture, there is something wild in everything specifically American, something that has not known the glossy, high-flown rhetoric, that theatricality of our bourgeois cultures, that has not been knitted in the gaudy finery of cultural distinction.

Here in the U.S., culture is not that delicious panacea which we Europeans consume in a sacramental space which has its own special columns in the newspapers—and in the people's minds. Culture [in the U.S.] is space, speed, cinema, technology. This culture is authentic, if anything can be said to be authentic. This is not cinema or speed or technology as optional extra (everywhere in Europe you get a sense of modernity as something tacked on, heterogeneous, anachronistic). In America, cinema is true because it is the whole of space, the whole of life that are cinematic. The break between the two, the abstraction which we deplore, does not exist: life is cinema.

That is why searching for works of art as sophisticated entertainment here [in the U.S.] has always seemed tiresome and out of place to me. A mark of cultural ethnocentrism. If it is the lack of culture that is original, then it is the lack of culture one should embrace. If the term taste has any meaning, then it commands us not to explore our aesthetic demands to places where they do not belong. When the Americans transferred Roman cloisters to the New York Cloisters, we find this unforgivably absurd. Let us not make the same mistake by transferring our cultural values to America. We have no right to such confusion. In a sense, they do because they have space, and their space is the refraction of all others. When Paul Getty gathers Rembrandts, impressionists, and Greek statues together in a Pompeian villa on the Pacific coast, he is following American logic, the pure Baroque logic of Disneyland. He is being original; it is a magnificent stroke of cynicism, naïveté, kitsch, and unintended humor—something astonishing in its nonsensicality. The disappearance of aesthetics and higher values and kitsch and hyper-reality is fascinating, as is the disappearance of history in the real and televisual. It is in this unfettered pragmatics of values that we should find some pleasure. If you simply remain fixated on the familiar canon of high culture, you miss the essential point (which is, precisely, the inessential).

The advertisements which cut into films on TV are admittedly an outrage, but they aptly emphasize that most television productions never even reach the "aesthetic" level and are, basically, of the same order as advertisements . . .[6]

If the U.S. has by now so thoroughly adopted TV as a general motif and model for everything, such that the U.S. has become at its deepest core a TV-reality, or a hyper-reality, society, then the question naturally arises as to what if anything might reverse or counteract this. To assess the nature as well as the strength of the possible restraining forces, we must turn to others.

In a delightfully clever and insightful book entitled *Why Nothing Works*,[7] anthropologist Marvin Harris gives us some valuable clues as to why the family, as a possible restraining force which could potentially counterbalance the negative effects of TV-reality, has virtually disappeared altogether. To do this, Harris examines the forces leading to the birth of the feminist movement. He traces the birth of feminism to the growing inefficiency of virtually all U.S. institutions over the course of the 20th century—especially the latter half.

As institutions grow in size, it is increasingly difficult for their members to relate personally and sensitively to one another, let alone to the whole of the institution itself. This growing inability produces breakdowns and inefficiencies first in communications and ultimately in the resultant end products and services of the institutions themselves. The consequence according to Harris is that in order to make ends meet, it became necessary for women to go to work in order to supplement the relative declining purchasing power of men's take-home salaries. In the beginning, women did not go to work because they wanted to, but because they had to. However, once employed and able to compete with men, they naturally balked and revolted against the countless inequities they encountered in the workplace. This, Harris contends, was the major impetus for the feminist movement.

One of the unfortunate and unintended consequences however was the breakup of the family. Because the issues involved in any discussion of feminism are inherently sensitive and hence the opportunities for misunderstanding are virtually endless, let us clarify our position

6. Jean Baudrillard, *Op. cit.*, p. 100.
7. Marvin Harris, *Why Nothing Works, The Anthropology of Daily Life*. New York: Touchstone, 1981.

as best we can and what we believe Harris's is as well. We are certainly *not* saying that the breakup of the family should be laid entirely
or solely at the feet of women, and that in addition the feminist movement should thereby be disbanded, or that women should return to
traditional roles. *We are saying nothing of the sort.* Instead, we are
saying that an unfortunate, unintended consequence of the women's
movement was a *contributing* factor to the demise of the family. If
anything, men can be faulted (or blamed if one wants to engage in
another form of the Blaming game at the societal level) more than
women for having created societies in which women are forced to
revolt.

In a pioneering study of some forty independent national cultures,
Geert Hofstede has isolated some of the major dimensions on which
they differ. One of the major dimensions is that of masculinity/femi-
ninity. To understand what the dimension is measuring, consider Table
1, which is reprinted from Hofstede.[8]

With a rank of twenty-eight out of forty the U.S. scores well
above average toward the masculinity end of the scale. What this
means is that unlike the Scandinavian countries, which according to
Hofstede's measurements score the lowest on the masculinity scale,
U.S. men have been far less willing on the whole than their counterparts elsewhere to participate seriously and actively in child-rearing. If
the family is a critical factor as a powerful counterbalancing force to
the driving forces behind a TV society, then if women are unable or
unwilling to fulfill the role of a primary care giver, then the slack must
be taken up elsewhere either through quality child care that is widely
available, or through mutual sharing of child caring by both men and
women. Japan which has the highest masculinity score of all the cultures surveyed by Hofstede is not dependent on men to fulfill this
crucial role because, among other things, the Japanese mother tradi-
tionally has been willing to spend up to five hours a day tutoring her
children after school so they can succeed in the highly competitive
Japanese culture.[9] This may help to explain why Japanese children still
manage to score near the top on worldwide educational achievement
tests even though one can make the case that Japanese society may

8. Geert Hofstede, "Motivation, Leadership, and Organization: Do American Theories Apply
   Abroad?" *Organizational Dynamics*, Summer 1980, pp. 42-63; see also Geert Hofstede, *Cultures Consequences*. Beverly Hills, CA: Sage Publications, 1984.
9. Merry White, *The Japanese Educational Challenge, Commitment to Children*. New York: The
   Free Press, 1987.

Table 1
The Masculinity Dimension

Feminine	*Masculine*
Men need not be assertive, but can assume nurturing roles.	Men should be assertive. Women should be nurturing.
Sex roles in society are more fluid.	Sex roles in society are clearly differentiated.
There should be equality between the sexes.	Men should dominate in society.
Quality of life is important.	Performance is what counts.
You work in order to live.	You live in order to work.
People and environment are important.	Money and things are important.
Interdependence is the ideal.	Independence is the ideal.
Service provides the motivation.	Ambition provides the drive.
One sympathizes with the unfortunate.	One admires the successful achiever.
Small and slow are beautiful.	Big and fast are beautiful.
Unisex and androgyny are ideal.	Ostentatious manliness ("machismo") is appreciated.

have an even worse junk TV system than we do.

The implication should *not* be drawn from the preceding that American women should therefore become more like Japanese women. To be completely honest, we have no adequate theories at the present to explain why one culture is more susceptible to the phenomenon of unreality than others. For instance, West Germany scores slightly ahead of the U.S. on Hofstede's masculinity index. At the same time, West German women also play a key factor in the work force, and yet, one does not see—at present—the same total drift toward unreality in West German society. This, of course, is no guarantee at all that it will not and is already not embarked on such a course as well. We may be currently in the unfortunate circumstance of having to invoke that which we are unable to understand as an explanation for that which we are trying to explain!

When it comes to individuals and to organizations, it is considerably easier to summarize the forces at work. In the case of the organizations we have examined, the driving forces contributing to major crises are the complexity and the tight-coupling that exist between the technologies that govern the modern world, many of which seem almost beyond our ability to understand, let alone control. In other words, the major driving forces are the increased complexity and shortened time frames within which all technologies now operate and the almost overwhelming number of factors which can affect their operation. At the same time, organizations largely attempt to control this complexity through the largely antiquated 19th century management structures that still permeate most institutions. In short, the technologies and systems which people are now charged with managing are highly complex and *interdependent*. At the same time, the management structures which are responsible for controlling these complex technologies are still founded upon the premise of *independence*, i.e., what we earlier referred to as the Fragmentation Game by which most professional functions and disciplines are organized. As a result, complex technology almost ridicules in the worst way possible the ways in which we have designed and operate contemporary organizations. The possible restraining forces are the new management structures that slowly but surely are coming into play, for example the case of the Brazilian organization Semco that we described earlier.

It is even easier to describe the main forces acting on individuals. The principal effect is akin to the experience of the destruction of the soul, the fragmentation or split of the "self" into so many separate pieces and bits that one literally experiences utter disintegration at the deepest levels of one's being. The driving forces responsible for this are many of the forces that we have previously described at length: the antiquated management and emotional structures that inhabit far too many organizations; the breakdown of the traditional institutions of society that would support and give comfort to individuals; the breakdown of widely shared societal myths that give meaning and purpose to life. Against all these powerful forces, the only means that society largely offers is that of individual self-help or therapy. While these to be sure are important, and much can be done by individuals to heal and to cure themselves, these fail to recognize that what is needed is the equivalent of therapy at the societal level.

To show why therapy at the level of the individual, as much as it can help, is no longer satisfactory, it is enough once again to refer to the results of psychotherapist Douglas LaBier,[10] whose practice is devoted exclusively to treating emotional problems associated with work. LaBier's results are strikingly similar to ours. Recall from Chapter 5 that LaBier has found somewhat paradoxically that those individuals who are emotionally "healthy" are often the ones who suffer most from their work experiences. Conversely, those who on the surface appear to suffer least are often among the sickest clients LaBier has treated. It is not enough to help and to transform individuals. As we have tried to show earlier, health can only truly flourish within those organizations and societies that are themselves somewhat healthy. While we do not have enough data to be absolutely sure about it, it appears from our research that Crisis-Prepared organizations promote an attitude such that individuals are freer and are even encouraged to partake of individual therapy. Even more, they are encouraged to use their newfound insights to better the organization in which they work.

NEW THINKING AND NEW FEELING

No matter which level of social reality to which we turn—the individual, organizational, or societal—we desperately need to evolve and to internalize new ways of thinking and of feeling if we are to address the serious issues we face. For instance, we have shown that individuals not only need to think differently if they are to prevent major crises from occurring and to manage better those that occur nonetheless, but also need to develop the capacity to handle feelings and emotions so that they and their organizations do not get caught up in playing destructive games. We also have shown that organizations need to develop different ways of restructuring themselves and of handling their emotional states as well. In a similar fashion, we believe that we need to investigate serious alternate designs for the delivery of TV programming, to mention only one area that is in need of serious reconfiguration at the level of U.S. society.

There is no question whatsoever of the great power of the electronic media to shape and to refashion attitudes. Thus, we have no doubts of the power that TV in particular played in overturning the dictatorial regimes of Eastern Europe. We do not thereby deny the fact

10. Douglas LaBier, *Modern Madness. The Emotional Fallout of Success*. Menlo Park, CA: Addison-Wesley, 1986.

that the media are and can be a powerful force for good in society or that isolated pockets of excellence already exist. But these are isolated exceptions. They do not represent the general fare with which we are bombarded daily. (Indeed, as one of the quotes at the beginning of the last chapter argued, the tearing down of the Berlin Wall was not the big media event the networks thought it would be perhaps precisely because we have become so jaded due to what we are presented with daily.)

The data, in other words, are "in" regarding the experiment called American TV. What we see is indeed what we get. Given the conditions under which the current system operates, there are no reasons to believe it will get any better or change significantly for the better.

If the prime purpose of the current system is to sell products and not to further the cultural life of the nation, then the current system serves this goal perfectly. In fact, given the current system, there are no financial incentives whatsoever for it to improve substantially. For to improve would almost surely mean to cut down substantially on consumption behavior. If this is indeed correct, then the only alternative is to design and to move toward another system. While the purpose of the present book is not to lay out the design and implementation of a new system in detail, for this in itself is a fitting topic for a whole study, we can at least allude to some of its most critical features.

An important beginning surely consists of the reconfiguration of the news at every level. If we have learned that the news is too important to be left *in its entirety* to the vicissitudes (games) of a consumerist society, then we have also learned that news is too important to be left completely in the hands of government agencies. However, there is no reason why these two extremes are the only options that are open. Other *capitalist* societies (and the stress is indeed on the word "capitalist") such as Great Britain and the Netherlands have learned how to fashion and to mix government-supported programs and channels with commercial ones.[11] True, these systems are currently experiencing significant difficulties of their own. But then as we have seen in the case of General Motors and the American automobile industry in general,

11. Jeffrey B. Abramson, F. Christopher Arterton, and Gary R. Orren, *The Electronic Commonwealth, The Impact of New Media Technologies on Democratic Politics.* New York: Basic Books, 1988.

the design of social systems is a continual, ongoing process. It is never finished. This is precisely the point of our discussion of the need for all organizations to continually reassess their basic assumptions and principles on which their design and operations rest. The main point remains: If one wishes a certain desired outcome, then one has to design that system or systems to improve the chances of obtaining it.

Part of the impetus for such a design consists in the realization and acknowledgment that the so-called "free TV system" in the U.S. is not in fact really free at all. If one factors in the costs of advertising into the final cost that consumers pay for products, then it has been estimated that America's TV system costs the typical viewer some eight times more than the government-supported TV systems of other countries.[12]

Americans thus have a clear choice: If they are satisfied with the current system, they can do nothing; if they are not, then they can insist that a range of alternative designs be commissioned and put before the people and their representatives for consideration. As we have seen, organizations can be extremely creative when they want to be. The creative energies of far too many organizations go into the playing of destructive games rather than directing that creativity to desirable ends.

Even these suggestions do not go far enough. Gore Vidal's notion that political campaign commercials or spots ought to be banished entirely from TV makes sense to us. They corrupt the political process by reducing a fundamental aspect of democracy to advertising commercials that actually work against the concept of democracy.

COSMIC TECHNOPHILIA

In the end, the most fundamental issue of all may be that technology and consumerism are so intertwined, allied, and inseparable in our culture that nothing may indeed be possible to break the domination they exert over every aspect of our lives. Worst of all, some not only welcome this domination, but even praise it as the next step in the evolution of "life forms." Under this view, "man" (referred to as carbon-based technology) is only one primitive life form out of many in the great chain of evolution:

12. Edward L. Palmer, *Television and America's Children. A Crisis of Neglect*. New York: Oxford University Press, 1988.

Why should silicon (i.e., computer-electronic) devices think of planets as home? Their natural habitat is the empty spaces between planets—ultimately, between stars. They float in these spaces like Portuguese Men-of-War in a warm sea. Their enormous-silvery arms, covered with solar cells, collect energy from the limitless tides that wash through space. Gravity would cripple those arms. Wind resistance would tatter the filmy sails. Dampness would film the polished skin. When *Voyager* left the solar system, it carried a message from mankind to the rest of the galaxy. Perhaps its true mission was to be the first of its kind to explore a future habitat.

Man was forced to create silicon devices when they did not exist. Having created them, he has been forced to exert his best energies in their service. In the forty years of their existence, they have already evolved further than carbon life in its first two billion years.[13]

Perhaps carbon man will pour himself . . . into silicon bodies. But with or without him, silicon devices will pursue their own destiny. There will be no hostility between the two forms—no galactic wars, no struggle for limited resources, no unplacable hostilities. The habitat of carbon man is earth, and his most precious resources are gravity, air, and water. The natural home of silicon devices is space, and their most precious resource is energy.

Carbon man may well continue to breed, as all other animals have continued to breed in utter indifference to their status on the evolutionary scale. Perhaps earth will come to be a kind of galactic game preserve in which rare species, of which carbon man is one, are protected as elephants are now protected in Kenya. Perhaps earth is already a game preserve. This idea is called the "zoo hypothesis" by scientists looking for intelligent life elsewhere in the universe. It is used to explain the odd fact that no signs of life have been detected, even though common sense and elementary statistics suggest there is lots of intelligent life in every direction . . .[14]

Silicon life will be immortal. The farthest reaches of space

13. O. B. Hardison, Jr., *Disappearing Through the Skylight, Culture and Technology in the 20th Century*. New York: Viking, 1989, p. 337.
14. *Ibid.*, p. 339.

will be accessible to it. For silicon beings, 100,000 light-years will be as a day's journey on earth, or, if they wish, as a refreshing sleep from which, when the sensors show the journey is over, they will awaken with no sense of passage of time or—what is the same thing—with visions "Of what is past, or passing, or to come."[15]

Humankind can barely manage the technologies it has invented thus far, and yet, it has the hubris to imagine wonderful new technologies that will demand even greater management skills if we are not to be overrun even further! Or perhaps all these marvelous inventions are instead expressions of the feeling that humankind has given up, that at some level it knows that it has invented technologies it can no longer master, and has thus elevated its inventions to the status of gods. Certainly as one reads passages like the preceding, one cannot help but reflect that they contain attributes that were once reserved for the deities. All those qualities that were once revered as the highest aspirations of humankind have now been projected onto our machines.

What is not presented as an alternative in such passages, perhaps because it seems so impossible to us at this point in history, is the possibility of human culture evolving and changing on a scale previously unexamined. What seems called for is no less than a revolution in human culture, a change in human consciousness if we are to manage the range of marvelous machines we have invented. Perhaps because the task is so daunting it is infinitely easier to imagine our marvelous machines evolving faster and better than us so that our changing is no longer a requirement. And yet, unless the human species is willing to write itself off entirely, this is precisely the task to which our best minds and efforts should be turned. If we can invest so much of our precious energy in machines, does not the human race deserve at least one more attempt at putting that energy back into itself?

One of the cornerstones of the great German philosopher Immanuel Kant's system of ethics was the notion that man was never to be treated as a means but always to be considered as an end. This notion was fundamental to Kant's concept of a kingdom of ends such that it constituted the basis for ethics. Those who see humankind as merely "carbon technology," whose prime purpose is not merely to be re-

15. *Ibid.*, p. 348.

placed by "silicon-based technology" but to further the very evolution of machines, do not endorse Kant's notion, to put it mildly. But herein lies the full force of Kant's concept: If one of the hallmarks of humanness is precisely the capacity for a moral imagination, what then is the moral basis for humankind's serving as a means to machines?

In some of the most deeply poetic lines ever written by a philosopher, one thing is clear. It is all the difference in the world. It is the difference between those such as a Kant who can see the "fact" that man is able to see and quest after the "moral law within" as the quintessential defining quality of what it means to be human as opposed to those who see outer space as the ultimate frontier:[16]

> Two things fill the mind with ever new and increasing admiration and awe, the oftener and more steadily we reflect on them: The starry heavens above me and the moral law within me. I do not merely conjecture them and seek them as though obscured in darkness or in the transcended region beyond my horizons: I see them before me, and I associate them directly with the consciousness of my own existence. The former begins at the place I occupy in the external world of sense, and it broadens the connection in which I stand into an unbounded magnitude of worlds beyond worlds and systems of systems and into the limitless times of their periodic motion, their beginning and their continuance. The latter begins at my invisible self, my personality, and exhibits me in a world which has true infinity but which is comprehensible only to the understanding—a world with which I recognize myself as existing in a universal and necessary (and not only, as in the first case, contingent) connection, and thereby also in connection with all those visible worlds. The former view of a countless multitude of worlds annihilates, as it were, my importance as an animal creature, which must give back to the planet (a mere speck on the universe) the matter from which it came, the matter which is for a little time provided with vital force, we know not how. The latter, on the contrary, infinitely raises my worth as that of an intelligence by my personality, which the moral law reveals a life independent of all animality and even of

---

16. For a more contemporary thinker who is also highly sympathetic to Kant, see, for example, William Barrett, *Death of the Soul, From Descartes to the Computer*. New York: Anchor Press, 1986.

the whole world of sense—at least so far as it may be inferred from the purpose of destination assigned to my existence by this law, a destination which is not restricted to the conditions and limits of this life but reaches into the infinite.[17]

A FINAL NOTE

Because on the whole we are so sympathetic to Baudrillard's brilliant theses, it is all the more critical to point out those areas in which we disagree. We agree with Baudrillard that, among many, humankind has passed through at least three distinct phases that have influenced greatly its concepts of reality. The first may be called the Phase of Nobility. In this era, things are authentic. How things look is in fact what they are. Thus, the dress, furniture, and estates of the nobility are not only authentic but are precisely what they are because they are strictly confined to and thus mark off unambiguously one class from another. To appropriate the symbols of another class is not only to commit a social faux pas but literally a crime. To copy without permission, even with it, is to make a forgery, a fake. Because there is still an underlying reality, the terms "forgery" and "fakes" have meaning.

With the industrial revolution, one reaches an altogether different situation. In the strict sense of the term, there are no fakes any longer because everything is. The endless repetition of identical products rolling off an assembly line is akin to the industrialized production of identical fakes.

With the ability to manufacture endless images and illusions (whether they be "people," e.g., politicians, celebrities, or contrived landscapes, i.e., malls and cities), to transmit electronically enhanced and doctored messages and events, we have entered the most ominous phase of all. This is Baudrillard's age of *simulacra*.[18] There is no longer any "reality" beneath the face, image, message, or symbol. Everything is or threatens to be a simulation of a prior simulation if indeed "things" can even be distinguished from one another at this point. For example, former President Reagan is a simulation of an actor simulating a president of a society that is itself a simulation of an 18th century ideological view of the world.

17. Immanuel Kant, *Critique of Practical Reason*, translated by Lewis White Beck. New York: Bobbs-Merrill, 1956.
18. Jean Baudrillard, *Simulations*. Columbia University, New York: Semiotext, Inc., 1983.

This endless chain of simulations of simulations is what Baudrillard calls hyper-reality. As sympathetic as we are to Baudrillard's thesis, as much as his incredible insights illuminate even additional hidden invisible "truths" of so-called advanced societies, we must nevertheless take exception to the full set of inferences or conclusions he derives. The end link of hyper-reality is not necessarily more hyper-reality or simulations but crises, indeed mega-crises. This is not to deny that the end link of hyper-reality is also not additional hyper-reality. The point is that reality, hyper-reality, and mega-crises can be—indeed are—present simultaneously. In fact, the simultaneous coexistence—if not mutual causation—of reality, unreality, and mega-crises is perhaps the most distinctive feature of our age. Thus, try as we might to conceal the truth, to manipulate reality solely to our purposes, humankind never has been able or will be fully able to banish reality completely or successfully.

In our day and age, the end result of our illusions come back to haunt us in the form of mega-crises. It is undoubtedly true that the perception of crises and their imagined control is filtered through computers and the media for a growing number of those who live in so-called "advanced societies," especially those who pretend to "manage" large institutions. For such individuals, the "reality" of crises may have become essentially and largely indistinguishable from their electronic renderings. However, for the most vulnerable in our society—the poor, the homeless, blacks, young children—it is a far different matter. The poor who lived in the squalid slums immediately surrounding Union Carbide's plant in Bhopal, India, experienced firsthand the direct effects, the "reality," of modern technology.

If the environmental movement does not turn into but yet another electronic media event (Earth Day, after all, has already come and gone with the swiftness of another slick event), then it might just have the power to shake everyone—rich and poor, old and young, conservative and liberal—back into collective reality. The difficulty is that threats such as global warming are not only complex, and as such, can only be understood through highly complex computer models which thus remove the phenomena from the direct understanding of people. Nonetheless, enough of us can still see because we experience directly every day the degradation of the environment, so that we might just be moved to shake ourselves free from the devastating effects of *inappropriate* technology that has been unleashed on a global scale.

In the end, the questions are: Does the earth, i.e., nature itself, still beat strongly enough within us so that the illusions of the hyper-real world cannot dampen its pulse? Or, what new mega-crises will it take to shock us back to reality?

. . . What shall it profit a whole civilization, or culture, if it gains knowledge and power over the material world, but loses any adequate idea of the conscious mind, the human self, at the center of all that power?[19]

19. Barrett, *op. cit.*, p. 166.

Appendices

CHAPTER 8

Box 1

Stanley Maisler, "Coming Home to Find a Smug, Scared America," *Los Angeles Times*, June 4, 1983, Part V, p. 3.

The cornucopia on a U.S. supermarket shelf . . . numbs the sense of choice. A shopper searching for salad and dressing must now chose among Honey French, Italian, Creamy Italian, Zesty Italian, Robust Italian, Blue Cheese, Thousand Island, Caesar, Sweet and Sour, Ranch, Buttermilk and Herbs, Celery Seed and Onion, Dill and Lemon and more.

There are at least eleven brands of dog food. Even bagels come in a host of flavors: garlic, onion, rye, pumpernickel, honey, wheat, bran, sesame, poppy, cinnamon raisin—and plain.

Yet this dazzling display of abundance comes in enormities of shopping malls that proliferate around cities like pillboxes on guard against style and beauty. Such clusters of concrete existed two decades ago but never in such size and strength. They symbolize the sprawl and flight that makes spiritless U.S. cities so different now from the vibrant, lovely towns of Europe.

No memory prepared me for the awfulness of American television commercials—almost every message loud, every scene frenzied. Any touch of subtlety vanishes with constant repetition. Only a masochist would sit through them with any pleasure, the way most people watch commercials in Paris. Sophisticates regard commercials in France as works of art; the best-known French movie directors make them.

No memory prepared me for the mindlessness of the 1988 presidential campaign. I had just covered the French presidential elections where the televised debate was sharp and meaningful, campaign speeches long and thoughtful, the differences between candidates clear and philosophical. France allows no political spots on television. Campaign managers do not mold strategy around sound bytes.

Television has created a vacuousness in American public life. Soon after arrival in Washington, I was entangled in several misunderstandings. While I thought I was arranging lengthy interviews with officials, they assumed I was setting up quick phone calls to catch pithy quotes. Television had instilled the idea that reporters needed no more than 15-second bytes.

"You are an anachronism in American journalism," said Marvin Kalb over dinner in Cambridge one night. The director of Harvard's Joan Shorenstein Barone Center on the Press, Politics and Public Policy explained, "You actually want to interview somebody."

Experience overseas taught me that no other people have the same control over their destiny as Americans. American democracy allows the people more rights than any other political system and more input—either through the power of public opinion or Congress—into government . . .

Box 2

Thomas B. Rosenstiel, "Viewers Found to Confuse TV Entertainment With News," *Los Angeles Times*, August 17, 1989, Part I, p. 17.

Americans are becoming increasingly confused about which television programs are news and which are entertainment, and they are divided over whether news programs should simulate or reenact real events, a *Times-Mirror* survey released Wednesday reveals.

Half of those surveyed believe "America's Most Wanted" is a News Program, and 28% believe it is entertainment, according to the *Times-Mirror* News Interest Index. The response is roughly similar for such programs as "A Current Affair" and "Inside Edition."

And, although the vast majority could not evaluate the two prime-time network news programs—"Prime Time Live" and "Yesterday, Today, and Tomorrow"—those who did were similarly divided over whether they are news or entertainment.

The survey found that Americans "very closely followed" only two news stories in early August—the Sioux City, Iowa, air crash, followed by 53%, and the apparent murder of Marine Lt. Colonel William R. Higgins, 49%.

The survey found that only 17% of the public could identify [Felix] Bloch [the State Department official suspected of being a spy]. Yet nearly double that number of the respondents, 33%, reported seeing an ABC news video reenactment of Bloch's alleged handing over of the secrets or said they had heard about the controversy caused by the unlabeled simulation.

Americans are sharply divided over whether news programs should fabricate or reenact events, even if the staged reenactments are clearly labeled as simulations. Of those surveyed, 49% approved the reenactments if clearly labeled, and 44% disapproved.

Attitudes toward simulations divide partly by age. Of those under age 30, 64% approve, compared with 35% of those 50 or older.

Box 3

Fred W. Friendly, "On Television: News, Lies and Videotape," *The New York Times*, Arts & Leisure section, August 6, 1989, pp. 1 & 27.

"What do you mean Felix Bloch might not be guilty—I saw him do it on television." The conversation took place at the Denver airport, and it was with a top editor of a major metropolitan newspaper. My friend, the editor, had heard . . . ABC's news correspondent John McWethy report that the United States diplomat Felix S. Bloch was under FBI investigation and had had his State Department passport revoked for allegedly passing top-secret information to a Soviet KGB agent. My friend was aware that the FBI had previously refused to comment, but what this experienced senior editor saw in the "ABC World News Tonight" was a videotape of "Felix Bloch" passing a briefcase to a "Soviet agent."

The videotape looked and sounded authentic; it was grainy, as hidden-camera film or tape often is. It was complete with an electronic time code, which law enforcement evidence usually carries, and there were even cross hairs in the picture to make it look more like genuine surveillance. My friend and, one can assume, millions of Americans perceived the briefcase sequence as an impressive ABC news scoop.

Peter Jennings, the network anchorman, introduced the report as an ABC exclusive, together with a lead-in containing one line of poetic irony: "We begin with a harsh reminder that secrecy sells." That was followed by the superimposed label "Exclusive." It was exclusive, all right. These startling and dramatic pictures were a fraud; a fraud perpetrated by ABC News, using an actor who resembled Mr. Bloch. It matters little that later that night a second feed of the ABC's news report carried a superimposed disclaimer— "Simulation"—at the top of the screen. Most viewers thought they were watching smoking gun evidence.

Box 4

Randall Rothenberg, "Messages From Sponsors Become Harder to Detect," *The New York Times*, November 19, 1989, p. E5.

Among its celebrity profiles and essays on male angst, the December issue of *Esquire* magazine offers an added treat for readers: The winner of the Absolut Story Contest.

The short story, which includes a previously supplied sentence with the name of the vodka, is clearly identified as an advertisement. Equally clear is the notice that the winning tale was selected by a panel of *Esquire* editors and executives of Carillon Importers—a collaboration that violates guidelines established in 1982 by the American Society of Magazine Editors restricting editorial involvement with a publication's advertising.

The advertisement is the latest indication that the once sacrosanct line separating editorial matter and advertising in print, broadcast in entertainment media is eroding, a victim of media companies struggling for ad revenues in a stagnant market and advertisers only too eager to exploit their weaknesses.

For television, marketers have found an equally powerful and subtle tool in video news releases, commercials that are disguised as television news segments and that run primarily on news programs, often identified only as "file footage."

But it is print, where journalists have long prided themselves in the sanctity of the church-state separation between editorial matter and advertising, that commercials have encroached most successfully. "Church and state are breaking down," Paul DuCharme, the head of print media at Gray Advertising, told an advertisers' conference in September.

Family Circle magazine this year published stories about the renovation of an old house by Martha Stewart, contributing editor of the magazine and a paid consultant to the K-Mart Corporation. The retailer purchased all the advertising space surrounding the features. Ms. Stewart, who used only products available at K-Mart in the work, appeared in the company's television commercials endorsing some of the products.

"I think the situation is worse today than in the past," said John Mack Carter, the editor of *Good Housekeeping* and a publishing industry veteran.

He attributes the blurring of the distinction between advertising and editorial content to a growing tendency for magazines to fend off requests for rate discounts by offering advertisers merchandising support or other forms of "added value" to the space they buy. A common form of added value that publishers give advertisers are the department store signs with pictures of a product "as advertised in" a magazine. But, Mr. Carter said, "sometimes the added value indeed involves more pressures on editors to participate in the advertising."

So acceptable have these editorial-advertising hermaphrodites become that several well-known authors, and including David Halberstam and John Kenneth Galbraith, accepted an average of $60,000 each to write short books on socioeconomic subjects sponsored by, and including ads for, the Federal Express Corporation. The books are published by Whittle Communications, a Tennessee company that specializes in new forms of sponsored journalism, notably Channel One, the advertiser-supported in-school television news program that has stirred the ire of many educators.

Box 5

Ellen Goodman, "It's Escape Mode for the U.S.," *Los Angeles Times*, March 6, 1990, pp. B7.

In Germany, every citizen is talking about reunification. In America, I replied [to my friend], they want to know who split first and whether there was a younger woman involved.

It occurs to me that in some perverse way, trivial pursuit has become the serious pursuit of our country. Once we were told that the business of America was business. Now our business is escapism.

Entertainment is our most important product. Were Dustin Hoffman to remake *The Graduate* someone would tell him a new password to success: not "plastics" but "videos."

Across the world, people look to America, not for leadership or enlightenment, but for a good time. In the late 18th century, Americans inspired the French hit credo "Liberty, Equality, Fraternity." In the late 20th century, we inspired the French with the hit movie: *Sex, Lies, and Videotape.*

Japan sends us cars. We send them baseball and theme parks.

Is it any wonder that it becomes harder and harder to separate news from gossip, the serious from the frivolous, Rob Lowe from Lee Iacocca, Trump the airline from Trump the divorce? We've become the paid comic, the hired storyteller, the world's great escapist. The new slogan of the American Way is: Let Us Entertain You.

Box 6

Ronald Brownstein, "Intellect Is Out in U.S. Politics: Unlike Europeans, Americans Prefer Pragmatists Over Philosophers and Artists for Elective Office. But Should They?" *Los Angeles Times*, March 4, 1990, pp. A1 and A22-A23.

In this country by contrast [with Europe], serious writers probably have less influence in political debate than radio talk-show hosts.

"There is quite a different tradition in Europe in relation to its intellectuals than in the United States," said playwright Arthur Miller. "We regard fundamentally the writer as an entertainer. He is there in order to divert and amuse us rather than to act as a moral leader of some sort."

It was not always so. Many of the Founding Fathers were well-read, graceful writers and earnest amateur philosophers—intellectuals by any definition.

By the early 19th century, the suspicion of intellectuals and government had fused with the populist revolt against the dominance of the young nation's politics by wealthy landowners—not incidentally the people who had the most time to stay abreast of the latest developments in science and literature. Through most of the rest of the century, populist and then business values dominated Washington and pushed intellectuals away from power.

But the public has been far less willing to embrace intellectuals as fit for elective office. What the late historian Richard Hofstadter ornately described 30 years ago as the tradition of "anti-intellectualism in American life"—the populist suspicion of effete, impractical "eggheads"—remains a powerful current in American society today.

"We are a pragmatic society," said Richard H. Pells, an intellectual historian at the University of Texas at Austin. "We distrust ideas, ideology. We distrust people with visions, we distrust abstractions."

Box 7

Fred W. Friendly, "On Television: News, Lies and Videotape," *The New York Times*, Arts & Leisure section, August 6, 1989, pp. 1 & 27.

The ABC news incident of July 21 [i.e., a simulation of the alleged spy Felix Bloch passing secrets] is not only an outrageous demonstration of shameful journalism, it also brings the national focus to ever increasing sins of irresponsible reporting shared by many other news organizations, print and broadcast. First, there is a sloppy habit of permitting "unnamed sources" to spread undocumented attacks on a wide variety of public officials and others who have neither been formally charged nor indicted.

The on-air apology that Mr. Jennings delivered four days later for not labeling the simulated portion of the piece as clearly as was possible certainly was called for—but for him simply to have dismissed ABC's news action as a "production error" is to miss the larger point. The dialogue created by this lamentable lapse of standard at ABC News could prove worth the hassle, since it occurs at a time when television news in general is going through an identity crisis. Is it to continue to be a serious and responsible instrument of communications operating under thoughtful guidelines, or is it to be twisted into an electronic carnival, in which show-biz wizardry and values obscure the line between entertainment and news? To fuzz that distinction further is to ignore the opportunity this ABC News incident brings into sharp focus.

As Ed Murrow used to say, "There will always be some errors in news gathering, but the tricks that microphones, cameras, film [and videotape] make possible must never be contrived to pass off as news events that were fabricated to document an event that we missed or which may never have happened."

There are those who have dedicated their lives to the principle that a fake sound effect, whether just a dubbed-in howitzer blast in Korea or Vietnam, or canned applause at a political rally in Des Moines, is blatantly dishonest. To simulate reality may be acceptable on a Hollywood film, but such practices have no place in serious broadcast journalism, where what you see is precisely what happened or "we don't show it," as Ed taught us all.

The ABC News offense cannot be excused as dramatic license, as some defenders have suggested, akin to animation of a moon landing or an artist's rendition of a courtroom during a trial where cameras are not permitted. Such reasoning ignores the obvious fact that the public recognizes the animator's or the artist's pen is recording an impression. In this exploding television age, most landmark events have been recorded: Joe McCarthy and Joe Welch were captured on film in 1954, the Watergate hearings were recorded on videotape in 1973 and the student demonstrations in Tiananmen Square were broadcast live via satellite earlier this year. No one and no history can honestly doubt that these events ever happened just the way they did.

I have always opposed the concept of docudramas, especially when it involved journalists and news-division imprimaturs. Today, the docudrama, blurring reality news and contrived theater, is everywhere. The actor who played Oliver North in a recent docudrama could not help but show the former White House aide in a false light, because neither he nor the screenwriter was privy to actual conversations involving the president and the director of the CIA and Colonel North. To those of you who see him as a heroic figure or as a villainous manipulator, the contrived dialogue remains as a lasting impression of the facts.

In the final analysis, the responsibility rests with top management. The current chief executive officers of the major networks have emerged from the ranks of money managers and manufacturers who are not steeped in the tradition and standards of broadcast journalism. In William Saroyan's classic play, *The Time of Your Life*, one of the characters muses, "No foundation. All the way down the line."

Box 8

Don Kowet, "Documentaries Witness a Revival," *Insight*, October 30, 1989, pp. 46-48.

[Av] Westin [an ABC executive once in charge of long-format programming] argues that "Americans have been video-educated" by sitcoms and cop shows "to expect emotional payoffs every twelve minutes. A cliffhanger, a car chase and then cut to a commercial. Not only can the audience compare your broadcast with the entertainment shows in the same time slot, but with the slickly produced commercials right in the middle of the program," he adds. "The payoff-every-twelve-minutes format is so dominant that the news divisions have been forced—not unwillingly, in many cases—to adopt it."

The payoff for network news divisions is that news programming, once regarded as a company loss leader, now is the second most popular form of programming on television, according to CBS researchers. Last year, news broadcasts trailed only sitcoms in the ratings race, besting serial dramas, action shows and general dramas . . . "Now there is only one priority for news departments: make money."

"What we're seeing is programs that cater to the lowest-common-de-nominator taste of the American people," adds [Marvin] Kalb. "And that's not what the network news departments ought to be doing."

"You can no longer do what the networks used to do, which is to present news programs with disdain for the audience," [Paul] Greenberg [NBC senior executive producer in charge of news hours]. "In order to hold a prime-time audience, you've got to entertain as well as inform, by making the show exciting. The only worthwhile shows are the ones people talk about the next day at the breakfast table or around the office water cooler."

But critics insist that the most serious prime-time news programs may be CBS's fictional "Murphy Brown." They suggest several related reasons for the traditional documentary's decline, not the least of which is that each of the networks has lost some of its independence after being taken by a media titan.

Using lively production techniques, these new programs have also become perfect vehicles to showcase a network's most promising talent, particularly its women. Glamour girls such as [Connie] Chung, Norville, and Shriver share vital statistics similar to those of the sexy actresses who lure large prime-time entertainment audiences.

[Pamela Hill, a former ABC vice president] adds, "I'm not optimistic about real documentaries ever coming back."

Box 9

Thomas B. Rosenstiel, "Reporters on TV, Is Stardom Weakening the Press?" *Los Angeles Times*, April 26, 1989, pp. 1 & 19.

". . . The *Chicago Tribune* now employs a media consultant to coach and promote its Washington correspondents for television. *USA Today* regularly features its newspaper reporters as experts on its TV show, hoping that one helps sell the other. And when one newspaper chain recently asked columnist Jack Germond to recommend candidates for Washington's Bureau Chief, it noted that being a regular on TV was a prerequisite.

"When that happens," said Germond, "things have clearly gotten screwed up."

Some reporters fear the culture of the TV programs may even be changing the basic values of print journalism, downgrading by degrees the traditional skills of reporting, neutrality and objectivity while elevating the skills that get one and keep one on TV—a knack for asserting opinions, talent for thinking in sound bytes rather than nuance, and a skill for honing an attention-getting public persona.

"It's a whole new world," said Sue Ducat, producer of "Washington Week in Review." "The whole phenomenon of the journalist realizing that visibility can boost their careers in a number of ways has really taken off."

Ducat, in fact, is innundated with requests from print reporters who want to appear on the show. Some sent her same-day faxes of their stories; others deliver videotapes of their previous TV appearances.

So powerful is television's invisible wave, the medium changes not only the message but also the messenger.

There is also one other problem with the rise of the shows and their influence, said [Charles] Broder of the [Washington] *Post*. The programs are helping to blur the line between journalists and the officials they cover, he says. This raises the danger of journalists allowing themselves "to become androgynous Washington insiders," as he put in a speech last December, "all of us seeking and wielding influence in our own ways."

Everybody has a right to be on television if their programming commands an audience and the content doesn't, as they said in a prior century, frighten the horses.

If the purists want to fret over something, they should address the troubled future of television news.

Box 10

Jack Solomon, *The Signs of Our Times*. Los Angeles: Jeremy Tarcher, Inc., 1988, p. 139.

The blurring of ad and program is a relatively recent feature in the short but active history of television. It was easier to tell the difference between a Gleem commercial and "Leave it to Beaver" than it is to see the difference between a spot for Coca Cola featuring Max Headroom and the program itself. The implications here are disturbing; for in the blurring of the lines between product pitches and program drama we can see a reflection of a society that has become so saturated with commercialized illusions that it can't tell the difference anymore. The United States is becoming one big television show, with actor-presidents and performing executives (note how often Lee Iacocca appears in Chrysler commercials) all underwritten by corporate contributions.

Box 11

Van Gordon Sauter, "In Defense of Tabloid TV," *TV Guide*, August 5-11, 1989, pp. 3-4.

The spectrum of human experience and emotion is arrayed before us on [the magazines on display at newsstands]. Now that service is increasingly available to us on television, which is replicating in our living rooms the scope of the old-fashioned newsstand. No longer is the delivery of news and information on television dominated by the programs produced under the imprimatur of the three networks or their affiliates.

The Colonel Blimps in . . . [Washington, New York, and Cambridge, Mass.] denounce the "bad taste" displayed by these obstreperous newcomers. That's the code phrase for what really alarms these elitists: The popularization of news and information by people who don't wear the school tie of Establishment journalism. Not only that, these news people don't seem to have their story ideas or topics sanctioned by what's in the *Times* or the *Post*. Worse, they frequently display a shameless enthusiasm for stories that play to our visceral emotions. Sometimes through our prurient interests.

While the leaders arch their eyebrows and sniff the air for foul aromas at the mere mention of these programs, the real people out in the electronic village can't understand what all the fuss is about.

The public comprehends the difference between the nightly news and the likes of Sally Jesse Raphael or Oprah Winfrey or Maury Povich. One can watch a network news show (though not as frequently as in past years) and fully appreciate the skill and intelligence that went into it. But that doesn't mean one can't find a different kind of merit or enjoyment in some talk and tabloid.

It is really time for the critics to lighten up. These tabloid talk shows can be great fun. Sometimes they are relevant. Sometimes they are even—brace yourself—good journalism. The quick topic and motivated yes, a talk master can reveal the dimensions of significant human issues of clarity and reality beyond the grasp of print journalists.

Box 12

William A. Henry III, "Pssst . . . Did You Hear About?" *Time* magazine, March 5, 1990, pp. 46-51.

The real question is whether celebrity journalism or its subcategory gossip poses a genuine threat to taste and morals, or whether it is instead harmless airhead fun. The fear in the intellectual marketplace, as in the mercantile one, is always that cheap currency will debase good. Yet the truth is that even at the height of Trump mania, Bess mania, Malcolm mania or any of the other periodic explosions of silliness, those who wanted to know the weightier news of the world had no real difficulty in learning it. And seemingly as that front-page photo made him appear, Liz Smith's injection of herself into the Trump tempest was no more outrageous than Stanley's stunts in quest of Livingston, Nellie Bly's travel and impersonations, John Reed's reporter turned revolutionary in Lenin's Russia, or Barbara Walters' on air diplomacy to help launch the Camp David negotiations between Menachem Begin and Anwar Sadat. Journalists just like to grandstand.

The truly troubling thing about the resurgence of gossip is not what it displays about journalists but what it implies about their audiences.

Box 13

Isobel Silden, "A New Persona," *Emmy* magazine, January/February 1990 p. 9.

In reply to accusations that a new entertainment magazine [*Persona Video Magazine*] will discourage reading in the home even more, [the editors] Karen Jackovich and Charles-Terry Goldstein point to studies that show the average person reads only 15 minutes a day but watches television for four hours. Recently the only two magazines that have grown in single-copy sales are two entertainment publications, *People* and *Star*.

"Since people aren't taking time to read, we're giving them a visual opportunity to learn about celebrities," they state.

Box 14

Shawn Pogatchnik, "Kids' TV Gets More Violent, Study Finds: Saturday-Morning Cartoons Average a Violent Act Nearly Every Other Minute, According to a Three-Year Study by Annenberg School," *Los Angeles Times*, Calendar Section, January 26, 1990, pp. F1 and F27.

"Violence is imposing itself on producers and directors because it's cheap," [George] Gerbner [a professor in the Annenberg School of Communications at the University of Pennsylvania] said, contending that viewers cannot exercise the right to avoid "entertaining murders" and otherwise violence-laden programs.

"You can change channels but you do not have a choice. We are born into it," he said. "Like the wallpaper on the wall, you absorb its [TV's] pattern without even knowing it."

Gerbner noted that children's shows are rife with humorous abusive characters, the humor serving as "sugar coating" for destructive "messages of power." He emphasized that children watch an average of 27.3 hours of TV each week.

Box 15

Letter to the Editor, Dorothy Mikuska, Oakbridge, IL., *U.S. News & World Report*, November 27, 1989, p. 6.

Companies need to identify the true cause of the educational problems in this country so that they will not engage in mere Band-Aid programs such as those described in your editorial. The causes are the values and mixed messages that large and influential corporations send to our children. Through the media, businesses extol materialism, instant gratification, sex, violence, social acceptance and physical aggression, but seldom intellectual achievement, morality, social conscience, good interpersonal relations, long-term goal setting and hard work. For many children, there is little or no family unit to make even a feeble attempt to combat these destructive messages. Why should an impressionable youngster develop a love for learning when he sees the corporate world promote athletes or rock stars who earn millions without any educational qualifications? Why should education be important when the educational role models, his teachers, are viewed as overpaid if they earn $30,000 a year after teaching 20 years and having a master's degree? Why should a teenager do his homework when instead he can bag groceries or flip hamburgers at $5.00 an hour? Interestingly enough, he can then be exploited as a consumer by the very business world that panics when he lacks skills needed to perform the job! What do corporations really want?

CHAPTER 9

Box 1

Margaret Crawford, "The Malling of America," in *Variations on a Theme Park: Scenes From the New American City*. Michael Sorkin (Ed.), New York: Pantheon, 1990.

The West-Edmonton Mall [WEM], the world's first mega-mall, is the most recent holder of the *Guinness Book of Records* title, "Largest Shopping Mall in the World." (At 5.2 million square feet, it is nearly twice as large is the runner-up, South Coast Plaza in Orange County, which covers only 2.9 million square feet.)

From inside . . . [WEM] is virtually impossible to decipher. Familiar patterns of mall shops establish the only points of reference in a dizzying spectacle of attractions and diversions: A replica of Columbus's ship, the Santa Maria, floats in an artificial lagoon, where . . . submarines move through an impossible landscape inhabited by imported coral, plastic seaweed, live penguins, and electronically controlled sharks. Fiberglass columns crumble in simulated decay beneath a newly built Victorian iron bridge. Performing dolphins leap in front of a Leather World and Kinney's Shoes. Fake waves, real Siberian tigers, Ching Dynasty vases and mechanical jazz bands are juxtaposed under endless skylight atria. Mirrored columns and walls fragment these objects even further, shattering them into a kaleidoscope of images. Confusion is introduced at every level; the past and the future are collapsed into the present, barriers dissolve between originality and duplication, real and fake, near and far. History, nature, technology have all been equalized, processed into images by the mall's fantasy machine.

This implausible, seemingly random collection of images has been assembled with an explicit purpose: to buttress the mall's conceit, the encapsulation of the entire world within its walls. At the opening ceremony aboard the Santa Maria, one of the mall's developers, Nader Ghermezian, shouts in triumph, "What we have done means you don't have to go to New York, or Paris, or Disneyland or Hawaii. We have it all here for you in one place in Edmonton, Alberta, Canada." Publicity for the fantasy land hotel asks, "What country do you want to sleep in tonight?" offering theme rooms based not only on faraway places, Polynesia and Hollywood, and distant times, ancient Rome, Victorian England, but also modes of transportation from horse-drawn carriages to pick-up trucks.

These claims imply that the world of goods for sale inside the mall reconstitutes the abundance and variety of the world's available goods, offering a global choice.

The imperative [to consume] has become a central fact of everyday life in advanced economies. Although malls serve as privileged sites versus realization, the ethos of consumption has profoundly penetrated into nearly every sphere of our individual, family and public lives. This has widened the gap between the obvious delights offered through consumption and the unchanging worsening conditions of the world of production. As a result, consumption increasingly constructs the filter of consciousness through which we interpret both worlds . . .

For many individuals, the construction of selfhood is socially constituted through commodities. If the world is appropriated through an understanding of commodities, then personal identity begins to depend on one's ability to compose a self-image by selecting a personal set of commodities. This ethos of consumption is realized not only by the acquisition of material products, but through a supporting ideology supplied by professional advice, cultural products and social institutions. The formative influence of the family has been replaced by television, shopping malls and organized leisure activities, which convey attitudes that reinforce commodified self-definition. Traditional methods of learning how to cook, relate to others and adopt values have been supplanted by how-to guides, self-help books, magazine articles and television programs.

Commodities themselves consist of similarly fragmented attributes; they are bundles of objective and imputed characteristics and messages which change constantly. Since both sides of the relationship between consumer and commodity are composed of highly unstable elements, each side tends to collapse into the other. According to [William] Leiss,[1] "the realm of needs becomes identical with the range of possible objects, while the nature of the object itself becomes largely a function of the psychological state of those who desire it." In this fluid medium, the shopping mall performs a double task. First, by prolonging the period of "just looking," the imaginative prelude to buying, the mall reinforces the unstable interaction between the consumer and the commodity. Through a process of "cognitive acquisition, shoppers acquire commodities imaginatively by becoming familiar with their actual and imagined qualities. By mentally "trying on" products, they learn not only what they want and what they can buy, but also, more importantly, what they don't have, and therefore, what they need. Through this knowledge, a shopper can not only realize what they are but imagine what they might become. But since the attributes of the commodities are always changing, requiring the shopper to constantly redefine their knowledge, satisfaction always remains just out of reach.

Larger malls required more complicated techniques of simulation. The WEM has adopted another principle evident at Disneyland, the spatial compression of themes. The view from Main Street across an African Jungle and to the future allows discrete worlds to collide with an ease previously achieved only in the most speculative science fiction. WEM presents an even more fragmented juxtaposition of past and future, near and far, reality and fantasy. Eliminating the unifying concept of the "land" released a frenzy of free-floating images. If Disneyland's abrupt shifts of space and time suggested that changing realities could be as easy as changing channels on the television, the WEM, as one writer observed, is more like turning on all the channels at the same time. Again, the principle of adjacent attraction ensures that these images will exchange attributes with the multitude of commodities in the mall. This barrage of diverse images introduces a further level of complexification, multiplying and mixing the unstable nature of both commodity

1. William Leiss, *The Limits to Satifaction*. Toronto: University of Toronto Press, 1976.

and consumer needs until they reach almost fever pitch. The disorientation this produces poses the danger that over-stimulation may result in acute shopper paralysis and reduce profits. Separate spaces containing the hotel, water park and amusement area become essential, just furnishing necessary breathing room. Even the all-inclusive mall must acknowledge perceptual limits.

INDEX